Dark Justice

Five Stars

"Dianne is an inspiration, it takes lots of courage and determination to overcome the obstacles she was faced with. I am so happy she decided to share her story. I can't wait for part 2!!!"

Five Stars

"I love this book! Dark Justice tells a story that so many people have either heard of or experienced themselves. It's as if the author was having a conversation with me over a cup of coffee."

Five Stars

"Great book! Can't wait for the next one!"

DARK JUSTICE

Dianne Cooper

Wild Ivy
Publishing, LLC

© 2014 Dianne Cooper. All rights reserved.

No part of this book may be reproduced, stored in a retrieval system, or transmitted by any means without the written permission of the publisher or author.

2nd Edition published 10/5/2015 by Wild Ivy Publishing, LLC, Lawrenceville, GA

Any people depicted in stock imagery provided by Thinkstock are models, and such images are being used for illustrative purposes only. Certain stock imagery © Thinkstock.

Because of the dynamic nature of the Internet, any web addresses or links contained in this book may have changed since publication and may no longer be valid. The views expressed in this work are solely those of the author and do not necessarily reflect the views of the publisher, and the publisher hereby disclaims any responsibility for them.

ISBN: 978-0-9968140-0-3
ISBN (Ebook): 978-0-9968140-1-0

10 9 8 7 6 5 4 3 2

Wild Ivy
Publishing, LLC
www.wildivypublishing.com

Dedication

This Book is dedicated to William and Vallie. I miss you. RIP. Also to the most important people in the world, Benjamin, Juanita, and Alexis, the three people who always made me want more out of life. You are my motivators. I thank God for blessing me with you.

Prologue

I've just come from checking on a friend of mine who just had knee surgery. I've known her a long time. We were roommates at one time in a Federal Prison Institution. I've been here at Federal Prison Camp for three years now. I came here August 23, 2006. Before I came here I was in Tallahassee. I did ten years in that institution. I had so much fun there. Before I went there it was an all men institution. My nephew, Leroy Cooper was there. When he was there, I was in Danbury, Connecticut. I hated Danbury. I hated the snow and my roommate who was also my co-defendant. She used to get on my last nerve.

Before I was there I was in California. I had been in many different jails and detention centers from California to Georgia before entering into prison. Lord, it has been a journey. As I sit trying to write, I keep thinking back. See, I've been told by the Lord to tell my story. So this is what I'm doing.

Since I've been in this prison my mother, two sisters and my nephew, Leroy have died. The bad part of this to me is that I didn't get to go to their funerals. That hurt me really bad. I had to go through it alone. Yet I wasn't alone; the Lord was with me. If he wasn't, I would be a very crazy lady by now. Oh, I always believed, but, well let's say I tuned God out for a very long time.

At the moment, I've been doing time for eighteen years. I am fifty four years old. May 15, 2010 will be the first day of my nineteenth year. Yes, it's been a while. Well, let's get to how I ended up in prison with a forty to life sentence. I promise you, I didn't kill anyone!

Chapter 1

Joseph was supposed to have gone to buy some cigarettes. I guess I won't be smoking today. At least the kids don't understand how hard it is. I try not to let it show how unhappy I am. Shon kept telling me Joseph is on crack. Joseph is my husband. We've been married now for nine long, miserable years. It's not all Joseph's fault. I shouldn't have married him in the first place. The reason I married Joseph was because we had a daughter, Juanita. Well let back up a little.

My name is Dianne Cooper. At the moment it's Cooper because I got indicted under my ex-husband's name. He and I have three grown children; Benjamin Lashon, Juanita Richell and Alexis Marika. When we got married Alexis wasn't born yet. I had Benjamin (Shon) at age fifteen. My ex-husband was my first, if you know what I mean. I had Juanita at the age of sixteen. I broke up with Joseph because I didn't want any more kids. I got pregnant with Shon using a condom. It got stuck inside of me. Then I got pregnant with Juanita on birth control pills. It wasn't like he was taking care of the two kids we had. I was on welfare and my mama kept making me go back to school. I got tired and took the GED and passed the test.

Now back to my ex husband. I broke up with him and started dating this older guy, Henry Mobley. He was thirty and I was seventeen. I was smoking cigarettes, weed, and drinking my ass off. My road dawg at this time was Sandra Davis, my cousin. She was dating Marvin Corn. He was also older than she was. When I tell you we were balling out of control. I was giving my mother fever! She hated Henry and so did my sister, Linda. I dated Henry for four years. This particular day I was sitting on the front porch drinking a Red Bull. My two kids were in the front yard playing. I had them dressed alike. I was looking at them. By now I am twenty one. I said to myself, "It's time for me to slow down. I have a daughter. I don't want any other man over her. I need to go back and get her daddy and settle down. Become a family for my children." Right then I made up my mind that I was going to marry Joseph. It wouldn't be hard to take him from his girlfriend. His family and my family were close. His father, Reverend Cooper was my father, William Cooper's best friend. I'll never forget how they got in a fight over Joseph and me. My daddy found out I was pregnant. So he called Reverend Cooper to tell him that his son had gotten his baby daughter pregnant, and he was going to marry me. Reverend Cooper came over to the house and he and daddy started fighting. My daddy was drunk and so was Reverend Cooper. I told my daddy I didn't want to marry Joseph. I was only fifteen!

But anyway, Reverend Cooper ended up beating up my daddy.

My daddy ended up running me around the house because I told him I didn't want to marry Joseph. He had a broom running me around the house cursing me, telling me, "You're just like your mama! You are going to marry him, damn it. I mean it!" I told him "No I am not and I ain't like madear! I am just like you." My mama, who we call madear, came outside and told my daddy, "W. L., leave that child alone. She ain't got to marry him if she don't want to." He left me alone and turned on her. He told her, "That's why she's in the shape she's in now. You let her do what she wants to do." Anyway, I ended up marrying him six years later.

This is how that happened. One night my brother Larry and I went to this club on the hill, which is Joseph's side of town. As we were leaving, we passed this other little club and I saw Joseph and Angela sitting outside. She was sitting in his lap. I told Larry, "Look at that shit."

He said," Alright Rat, leave that man alone." I said, "I ain't leaving nothing alone. It ain't like he does anything for the children. I think I'll take him from her." Larry said, "Girl you are crazy." I hollered, "Joseph, come here." Then Angela hollered, "Who the hell she think she is calling you?" Joseph said, "Alright Dianne, don't start no shit!" I said, "I need to ask you something. Bring your ass here." Then Angela said, "He ain't your man. He ain't got nothing to talk to you about." I told her, "Shut the hell up. Bennie come here." I called him Bennie because his given name was Benjamin.

He told Angela, "She's my kids' mama. I'm going to see what she wants." Larry started laughing. I went and met him half way. He said, "Dianne what you want? Why you starting up shit?" I told him, "All I want to know is do you want me back?" He said, "Stop playing." I told him, "I am serious and if you do, then leave Angela alone and meet me in my mama's living room in two weeks." He said, "You're serious?" I told him yes. He started smiling and told me okay. He said, "You going to give me some tonight?" I said, "Sure. Tell Angela bye." He told Angela he had to go. I told my brother, Larry to go ahead because Joseph is going to take me home. He laughed and left. Joseph and I went to his house and did the do.

Two weeks later my sister, Elizabeth had a baby blue wedding dress made for me and some see-through shoes. I was married to Joseph in my parents' living room. My life went downhill from there. At the time, Joseph had a job. A month later we were living in the house I was born in, which needed a lot of work. So we moved to Sarasota, Florida and moved in with his mama's sister. Later, I got a job at a nursing home and he got a job at a concrete company. We left the kids with my mama when we left Waycross, GA. We went back to get them later. We moved into an apartment and I met this girl named Debra who showed me how to get furniture when people moved. We would go into the apartment and get the furniture that was left. I ended up furnishing our whole apartment.

Joseph and I would fight a lot. He would get drunk and boy, we would fight. I mean blow for blow. I started getting drunk to deal with him. One day he came home because he hurt his back. This meant he could no longer work. So I ended up being the head of the household again! I bought an old car. He would take me to work and pick me up as well. He had total control. To make it worse, somehow along the way I had fallen in love with my husband. I know the sex had a lot to do with it. Sex was the only good thing we had. Other than that, all we did was fight. I had black eyes, busted lips, and the whole thing. Yet he would tell me he loved me.

Now in all this, I heard at home that my father was very sick and they were trying to send him to a nursing home. My mama worked for a doctor who was a surgeon. He was willing to operate on Joseph's back. He had two ruptured discs. He had a fifty-fifty chance of being paralyzed. So we left the apartment and car to go back home.

My brothers, sisters and I took turns looking after our father, along with my mother. My dad had a tumor on his brain. He died trying to tell me something. My dad had called us in a little room and he was trying to write it, but his hands kept shaking. He started crying. I kept asking him, "What is it?" He couldn't seem to tell me. My son, Shon, was the only one who could understand my father. But Shon was too young to come in. By now, he was eleven. My dad died in my mother's arms. I just started running and hollering. My brother caught me and the nurse gave me a shot.

We stayed with my mama, then his mama and eventually moved

back in the house I was born in. After Joseph's surgery, we started repairing the house. While he was repairing the house, I didn't know he had gotten a settlement from his back. All I knew was the fighting was worse. I had gotten pregnant again, which I hated because I had just started going to school to be a RN and I was working at Ware Manor. Joseph didn't like it. He always said I thought I was better than him. I just wanted better for my kids. I loved them so much. We would fight a lot about them. He would always have my son on punishment, and I would take him off a lot of times. The bill money would be missing, and when I asked him, he would lie to me.

I came home from work one day and Juanita and Shon both were on punishment. Nita told me he had hit her and Shon. I asked him why and he went to cursing. "That's what's wrong with them. Every time I punish my own kids you come questioning me. I don't have to tell you shit." I asked him again, "Did you hit Nita?" He said, "Damn right." Before I knew it, I had picked him up and dumped him and was on top of him, beating him and talking to him at the same time. I told him do not hit my girls. He always said those children are going to tell you to kiss their ass. I told him, "If they do, it's okay. They kissed mine coming into the world." Then he called me a bitch. And I said, "You must be talking about the bitch you birthed." Then it would be another fight.

During this time Shon was fifteen and Nita was fourteen and Alexis was one and a half. We were sitting around watching TV. This is when Joseph was supposed to have gone to get some cigarettes. He came in the door and I asked him, "Where are the cigarettes?" He hands me a half pack of Salems. I was hot! I just took them, lit me one and went back to watching TV. He called Shon. He said "Ben Jr." Shon didn't answer. He said it again, "Ben Jr." Shon still didn't answer. Joseph grabbed Shon and tore his shirt. Shon jumped up and ran out of the house. I went behind him. What made me go, I don't know. All I know is that I did. Shon ran across the street to my mother's house and went into the back bedroom, which was my room, and got the .22 off the wall. It was my father's .22. On his way out of the room I caught him and got him to the floor and I said, "Shon, please." He was crying. He said "Ma, we don't need him. I told him that. I told you he is on crack. That's why he is always putting me on punishment. It's because I be seeing what he's doing."

I told him, "Shon, you can't shoot him. He's your daddy." Then he said, "Promise me you'll leave him." I was having a hard time keeping him down. I told him, "I promise." Then Shon said, "Ma you know daddy is going to fight you. Promise me you'll go buy you a gun." I told him, "I promise." Then I let him up and he put the gun back on the wall.

During all of this, my mama was standing there crying. So Shon stayed the night with her. What he was mad about was that I had just paid only half the light bill to buy him that polo shirt and his daddy tore it. So when I got paid, I went and bought my first gun. It was a

.25 automatic. That Friday when Joseph came home I had packed his little stuff in a garbage bag and had it by the door. He came in and I told him he had to go. He said, "What the hell you talking about? I ain't going nowhere." I told him, "Oh you leaving here. This is my house. Get your bag and get out." He looked at me, got his bag and drove off.

When he left, how about Nita, Alexis and I went to the store. Shon was standing behind me when I asked Joseph to go. The children were happy! Even Nita said, "We don't need daddy." I have to say, a kind of peace came over me. I stayed in that house for about two days, and then I moved out. I went back to live with my mama. When my sister, Linda and I was cleaning out the house, I found Joseph's settlement papers. All that time I was working and paying bills, taking that mess off him and trying to make it work, he had gotten a fifty thousand dollar settlement. He put it in the bank in his name and his daddy's name. He didn't have but a thousand left in his account. He was on drugs and had smoked it up. The next week, I filed for divorce!

Chapter 2

Two months passed and all I did mostly was work and stay home. After a while I started going to the bar after work with the girls. Sandra, Ann and me. We would get off work, stop off at the club, drink a beer and go home. Sometimes on Friday's we would make plans to meet up with each other. Mostly Ann would come and pick me up. This one particular night we were up on Oak Street at the club and this guy came over to ask me did I want something to drink. I told him, "No thank you. I already have a beer." Then he asked me did I want some cocaine. I told him, "Hell no! I don't do coke." He said, "What do you do?" I said, "Weed." He smiled and said, "Okay, I'll be right back." When he walked off, Sandra had a fit.

She said, "Bitch do you know who that is?" I told her, "Motherfucking no and I don't want to know." She said, "Bitch that's Diamond." Ann said, "He's the biggest drug dealer in this town! Bitch, get the coke and we'll use it!" I told her, "Oh hell no! You ain't using me."

When he came back, he dropped the weed on the table and he had a quart of beer. Then he said, "What's your name?" I told him,

"Dianne Cooper." He said, "You know Leroy?" I told him, "Yeah. He's my nephew." He said, "Ain't you married?" I told him, "Not really. I am in the middle of divorcing Joseph Cooper." He said, "You don't know who I am, do you?" I told him, "Am I supposed to know you?" He laughed and walked off. Sandra almost lost it. "Girl, you don't talk to Diamond like that. His last girlfriend, he pushed her out of the window and then paid her hospital bill." I told her, "So what's that got to do with me?" We got good and high that night. We balled out of control.

We left there and went to the dance they were having at the Spinning Wheel. I must have danced all night long. When I looked toward the bar I saw him watching me. When the dance was over, he came and asked me did I have a ride home. I told him, "No." Which I didn't. I was going to walk around to the taxi station and a catch a cab. He asked me, "Can I give you a ride?" I told him, "Yes, thank you." I got in the car. First, he stopped by his mama's house, and then he took me home. We didn't talk much. He asked me, "Do you have kids?" I told him "Yes, two girls and a boy." He asked me their ages. I told him, fifteen, sixteen and two years old. He told me he liked kids as long they're not his. He had the most serious look on his face.

He was dressed to the tee. I liked the way he stood and fell back on his legs, and he had this smile, oh my God! I called it a million dollar smile. I loved his smile. When I told Shon who had brought me home, he went crazy! He said, "Ma do you know who that is? Ma, that's

Diamond. Diamond Cluster. Ma, he got money." That boy started singing, "We in the money." He said, "Ma, you done hit it big!" I told Shon, "Boy, the man just gave me a ride home."

I had been messing around with this buster named James. His family was middle class. His sister had married a doctor. James was on drugs bad. But the sex was good. It was nothing serious. We worked at the same nursing home, that was about it. I remember one night we were at this motel. When I tell you we tore the people's head board up! That was the last time I was with James. I found out he was living with this girl and she had a child for him. Anyway, the next night Diamond showed up at my door. He asked me to ride with him, and I did. We were headed out toward Bailey Heights, the projects. He asked me if I was seeing anyone. I told him, "Yes. James." He burst out laughing. He said, "James? That nigger on drugs so damn bad, it ain't funny."

I said, "We just kick it. But that's it." That's when he said something that shocked me. He said, "Do you know I used to watch you when you were with your husband? I never could understand why you was with that nigger. God must have slapped you and woke you up and made you leave him." I just looked at him. He said, "Let me show you something."

We went to the middle of the street. I saw these young drug dealers doing donuts with my husband's car. He had rented out his car for crack. Diamond told me, "See, look at that. What do you need with him?" Then he called this guy to the car and told him, "Come here, man. I want to make her laugh." It was cold and the guy didn't have a coat on. He told this guy to "Bark like a dog and if she laugh I'll give you this twenty cent piece." The guy stood at Diamonds car window and barked, "Ruff, ruff." I didn't think it was funny. He told the guy, "No man, bark like a big dog."

The man barked again, "Ruff, Ruff!" He told the guy, "Here nigger." He gave him the crack and then went in his trunk and gave him a jacket. When he got back in the car he said, "Sorry ass nigger. I gave him that shit because he's my cousin." I couldn't believe him. "You made your cousin bark like a dog?" He said, "See the power you have when you sell drugs? People on that shit will do anything for it. That's how you get power over them. You got to be hard, baby. You can't be nice and make money!" The he turned to look at me. "So you gonna be my woman or what?" I told him, "Yeah, I'll give it a try." He reached in the back seat and gave me a pair of jeans, a herring bone gold necklace, a gold bracelet, and he had a carat and a half pair of diamond earrings. He pointed to the earrings and said, "You got to earn these." Then he put two hundred dollars in my pocket and took me home.

When I got home, Shon and his friend, Lenzy were there. They had looked out the window and had seen me get out of the car. Shon said, "Ma, how you get the biggest dealer? My mama all that!" I told him, "Boy he is just a man." Then I said, "I told him we'll give it a try." That boy acted like it was Christmas. "So ma, that's your boyfriend?" I told him, "Didn't I just say that?"

"So ma, he knows about us?"

I said, "Us who?"

"Alexis, Nita and me?"

I told him, "Is you crazy? I don't hide my children for anybody. We are a package deal. If you want me, you got to accept my kids." He just smiled and said, "Now that's my mama. See Lenzy, my mama ain't no joke. When it comes to us, she don't play." I told him, "You right. Anyway I am going to bed. I got to go to work. When I get off, I am going house hunting."

I hadn't seen my ex-husband for a while. Now this particular night, I went up on the streets. I was sitting at the bar in the club. Diamond hadn't come in yet. I was waiting for him. I was smoking a cigarette when I heard somebody say, "Hey Dianne, how you doing?" I turned, and Joseph was standing behind me. I turned around and said, "Hey yourself and I'm doing alright." He asked if he could sit down and I told him, Sure." All the while, I felt he was up to something and fear kind of set in on me. He sat down and had the nerve to ask me to buy him a beer! I told him, "Sure." He ordered his beer and I paid for it.

That man hit me so hard my earring flew off my ear and went behind the counter! He grabbed his beer and ran out the door. My head was ringing and the bar tender got my earring and handed it to me. I tell you Joseph had almost knocked my head off. My cigarette had fallen out of my hand. While I was still trying to focus, Diamond came in. He looked at me and asked me what was wrong. I told him what Joseph had done. He struck out after him. Diamond had Willie with him, his right hand man. He told Willie to get him and fuck him up. I told him, "Don't you touch him. That's my husband and this is between me and him. If you lay a hand on him, I'll blow your head off." He knew I carried a gun. I told him, "I shot him and I love him. What the hell you think I will do to you?"

He looked at me and gave me that smile. The smile I later fell in love with. He told me, "That's why I like you. You crazy as hell. Nobody else would ever tell me no shit like that." I told him, "I ain't nobody, I'm somebody." We ended up in the motel room that night.

The next morning we stopped and got breakfast. Then he dropped me off at my mama's house. As our relationship grew, we ended up having a lot of love and respect for each other. I had a bond with him that I've never had with anyone. We had something else I've never had with anyone: trust. I trusted him and he trusted me more than anyone. If I told him something, he knew it was the truth and he could believe me. If I didn't want to know the truth about something, I wouldn't ask him. Because if I did, he wasn't going to lie to me to spare my feelings. He would just tell me the truth. I loved him for that. He's someone I will always care about above all else. He is my friend.

I found a small house with two bedrooms, a large living room and a fireplace. I loved that! The day I was moving, Diamond took me to

Badcock's and bought me a new living room set, bedroom set, TV, stereo system and paid for the lights and water to be turned on. As for the phone and cable, I just had them transferred from my mama's house. We had two different phone and cable connections at her house. The kids and I moved into the house. The next day, Diamond came over. When I went outside to the car, the man had a trunk load of clothes and shoes. I asked him, "Why do you have all your clothes in the car," which was a stupid question. He looked at me like I was crazy! He told me, "What do you think? I'm going to take care of a woman that I'm not staying with?" I told him, "I don't need you to take care of me." The man said, "I pay rent here and I am going to live here."

That was that! After he moved in, he left and went up on Oak Street. I stayed home sitting on the bed looking crazy. Wondering what have I gotten myself into? I had no concept of what being a drug dealer's woman consisted of, but it didn't take me long to catch on. For one, I couldn't have a lot of friends. Nobody was to come over to the house, except family, or unless he brought a couple of his boys over. If I was in the living room when he came home with a couple of his boys, I had to leave and go to another part of the house. If I'm at the club, I can only dance with family or one of the boys.

Chapter 3

Diamond bought himself a new car, a Fifth Avenue. It was nice. When he came home with it, he asked me did I like it. He said "Baby, does it fit me?" I said, "Yeah baby." He looked at me and said, "No it don't. I need a sports car." My cousin lived in Florida. She had a house that was empty, so I asked her if I could rent it from her. She said, "Sure." So we moved on L Street right across from Hattie's mama. Hattie is the cousin I was renting from. It was a two bedroom, but I could make it to be a three bedroom. It had a fenced in yard, porch with a swing and a large backyard, and a washroom of course. Diamond had it remodeled. Then he got two dogs, Rottweilers named Zeus and Arco.

During this time, I had stop hanging out with Sandra and all of them. They were on that coke and I wasn't into that. I also had started working at Waycross Molden in quality control. I was mostly hanging out with this white girl named Angie. We became really close. She was going with this black guy who ran the club. I learned later that he used to beat her and he was married! Angie got away from him and ended up leaving town and getting married. I was very happy for her.

Diamond was happy too, because he didn't like her.

She had come to the house one night. He walked in and did not even speak to her. I knew he was mad. Angie knew it, too. She told me, "Look friend, I don't want to cause you any problems, so I'm going to leave." I told her "It's okay. I'll come to see you tomorrow." So I walked her to the car. I had to walk her because my dog Zeus didn't like too many people. The only person who could get close to him was me, Nita, Alexis and sometimes Diamond.

When she left and I went back in the house, Diamond asked me, "What's that white whore doing here?" I told him, "She came to see me, if that's alright." He told me, "No it's not. Please don't let it happen again." Then he went back out the door. So from then on, I went to her house. She had two kids, a boy and a girl.

He didn't come home that night. The next day after I came home from work, I was talking to my sister, Linda, on the phone and Diamond walked into the bedroom and threw a box at me. He told me, "See if it fit." I opened the box and there was a nine diamond cluster ring. I hollered on the phone and told Linda, "Girl I got a cocktail ring! I'll call you back." I put the ring on my finger and I couldn't do anything but smile. He smiled back and went back out the door with Willie.

I went over to Linda's house to show her my ring. She told me, "Fool that's not a cocktail ring, that's an engagement ring." I looked at her like she was crazy. That night Willie came over and told Diamond he had got jacked. Some guys from Florida had made him lay down on the ground and took his money and jewelry. That started a lot of mess. He started leaving me at home. He would have me a couple of bags of weed and some movies to watch while he went up on the streets. Then sometimes he would have me an outfit laying out on the bed. That let me know we would be going out. He bought all my clothes. He had good taste. He always wanted me in two colors. And he loved for me to have four hundred dollars in my pocket at all times. I must say, he was good to me and my kids. He didn't smile much.

One night, he went and got a lot of movies and told me to watch them and tell him about them when he got back. I sat there and smoked me a joint, then decided I did not want to watch no darn movie. So I went up on the streets. When I walked in the club, I heard somebody say, "Here she come." When I hit the corner it was this girl on the floor. Diamond had pushed her on the floor. She had been sitting on his lap. Neicey Doll was laughing, and she had the craziest laugh. She said, "Nobody won't be going to the motel tonight." She started laughing again.

Diamond looked at me and got up and said, "Baby what are you doing up here?" I asked him, "What is she doing on the floor?" He came towards me, talking about, "I asked you what are you doing up here?" I told him, "You know what the fuck? Here take your damn keys. I don't need this shit." I told him, "I got another set. I'm going to take my ass home." He went out the door before me. He beat me to his house. When I got there, my girls were up. I asked them, "Why are you all up?" They said, "Diamond woke us up and told us we were leaving." I got hot then, and went in my room to get my gun. I got it and pointed it right at his temple and asked him, "Who in the hell told you to wake up my kids, nigger? I'll blow your brains out." I clicked the gun and he had taken the clip out. I was so mad at him. He sat there froze. He couldn't even talk for minute.

When he could say something, he said, "She tried to kill me. Shit! She tried to kill me." I asked him, "What the hell did you do to my gun? Didn't I tell you about fucking with my gun?" I told the girls to get in Shon's car. I went in the room and got my clothes. I left the stuff he had bought me and went back to my mama's house and back to my old room.

My niece Tonya, Linda's daughter, called me the next day and said, "Auntie Dianne, what did you do to Diamond last night? He came out to the projects and was so nervous he couldn't even roll his joint. I had to roll it for him. He told me, "Your auntie crazy. She tried to kill me." I just laughed and told her, "He'll be alright." She said "Whatever you did, you messed him up. All he kept saying was that you were crazy." I didn't see or talk to Diamond for a week. I had gone back to work at the nursing home.

That next week I was coming through the street on my way home from work. I stopped and bought me a beer. I was sitting there and he came and punched a couple of numbers for records on the juke box.

He asked me, "Dianne look, can't we be friends?" I told him, "Sure, not a problem." He smiled and went out the door. James came and sat on the stool beside me and told me, "Dianne, don't believe that shit. Diamond ain't going to let you go. Trust me. Any man that try to talk to you, he's going to have a problem with Diamond." And he wasn't the only one who told me that.

A couple of nights later, I found out he was going with this girl maned Tamela Mack. She had six kids. I walked into the bar with my sister, Linda, and he's sitting there with Tamela and her brothers. He looked up at me and turned back and started talking to Tamela. I sat at the bar and ordered me a beer. I got my beer and went to sit in the back. I saw a couple of people that I knew; Sandra for one, and my cousin Jenny. So we got us a bag of weed and was chilling when Willie came over to the booth and said, "Diamond told me to bring you over to his house when you get ready to leave." I looked up at him and just said, "Sure, why not?"

Now he's sitting there with Tamela and got his do-boy telling me he wants him to take me to his house. He is something serious. So I went. When I got there, he wasn't there. He came about thirty minutes later. He comes in there smiling and talking about, "Baby I got something for you. Do you want a four day cruise to Jamaica?" I said, "Sure." He told me, "Your sister, Linda is going. I got a ticket and I'm going to give you some spending money."

I had to ask. I said, "Diamond, why you keep messing with me and you got a girlfriend?" He said, "Dianne, you don't believe I love you?" I told him, "No." He said, "If I had a rich woman, I would still keep you. You got to work tomorrow?" I told him, "Yes." He said, "Call in. I'll pay you for your day." So I did. And we went to bed. We didn't have sex, he just wanted me there. He did that a lot. He would call me just to be there. I would get in the bed and he would throw his arm across me and we would go to sleep.

One day he called me to get his dogs. Zeus was mine. I loved that dog. He used to sit on Nita's bed when she did her homework. Diamond said he didn't want me to mess with Arco. It didn't matter. Arco fell in love with me too! When his dogs would get out of the fence, he would call me. When they spotted my car they would run behind it and I would put them back in the fence. He had a fence around the yard and another fence in the yard with a doghouse.

About my car, one day I was sitting on the porch with my mama and Diamond pulled up in his new Trans Am. He asked me to go for a ride with him. I did. We ended up at the car lot. He said, "Get out of the car." So I got out. We were standing by his car and he pointed at another car and said, "What do you think about that car over there?" I said, "It's nice. But I like that blue Ford Probe over there." So he looked at it with that old serious look he gets. Then he said, "Ok." We went inside and he asked me, "What name you want it in?" I looked at him and then said, "Cooper." He told the man to put it in the name Dianne Cooper. Then he brought me the keys and said, "It yours." I drove off behind him. When I made it to my mama's house, he was there. I asked him "Why?" He told me, "Just because." I could never understand him until now, at this moment as I write this. And then he told me, "Now go to church!"

That next Saturday he called for me to go to church with him Sunday. He also would go to my church with me. He would call me over to go and pay his bills while I paid mine. Sometimes he would call me to come up on the block to go and get him something to eat, or pick up a bottle of Don. He still bought all of my clothes. The only thing that had changed was that I didn't live with him.

One night he called me over to his house. It seemed he had to go to jail in Claxton, Georgia and he wanted me to move into his house to take care of the dogs and handle his business. He had enough money in the house for me to take care of bills and everything until he got out. I didn't understand why he asked me. When I asked, he would say, "I trust you and we're friends." So I stayed over there. I went and got my baby girl, Alexis, to stay with me. He did about ninety days.

While he was doing time, Willie his first in command, so they called him, would check on me. When he called and asked me to come visit him, he had me to use his partner's car. I would drive down there to see him on the weekend. I didn't know until later that I was on display. He wanted me to visit so he could show me off to this guy named Jimmy West Taylor. You'll hear more about him later. He is nothing to play with. He had me to send this guy some money.

Anyway I was so glad when he got out. I was tired of his people riding by the house, making sure nobody was coming over there. They would even check to make sure I was at work! And I wasn't supposed to be his girl anymore. What kind of twisted mess is that? Well he got out and when he came home, I left and went back to my mama's house. He had the idea that I wanted to come back. That was something I didn't want. Like I said, my daughter Juanita couldn't stand him. I was not about to leave my daughter with my mama just to be with him! My kids came before any man, including my husband. He wasn't my ex yet!

Once I was dancing with Willie, Diamond walked through and he pushed me and Willie further apart, and we were fast dancing. Another time Willie was talking to me and he had his hand on my shoulder. Diamond walked by and pushed his hand off my shoulder and kept walking. By this time, I had found out that my seventeen year old son was calling himself selling drugs. I was too through. I asked him, "Shon, why would you want to do that?" He told me, "They put my daddy on crack, so I'm putting their daddy on crack." I couldn't say anything. I just looked at him.

The way I found out was Diamond told me. He said, "Baby I went and got Shon out of jail." Mind you, I didn't even know he had been to jail. He said, "If he gonna sell drugs, he might as well work for me. It don't make sense me going to get him out of jail and he's working for another nigger." I said, "You mean my son has been selling drugs?" He looked at me smiling and said, "You don't know anything do you? You are green." I told him, "No, I don't. Shon is the one who told me about crack." And then I said, "Why do you always tell me you going to work?" He said, "I don't be going to work. Don't worry about my job. You just go to work. The less you know about my job, the better off you are."

Shon and Diamond got very close. Diamond also had a lot of love for Alexis, my baby girl. He and Juanita did not get along too well. And I understood why. If any woman who had a dealer for a man thinks she's the only one, then she is crazy. I knew he had other women. That didn't bother me and as long as he gave me respect, I didn't have a problem. I mean it's not like I wanted to marry him. I liked things just the way they were. Besides, he was six years younger and no kids. My daughter didn't like it because she knew some of his girlfriends.

Chapter 4

One night about 2:00 a.m., I was asleep. My phone rang, and when I answered it was Diamond. He told me, "Baby come to the hospital. I need you to drive me home. I've been shot. I'm sending Duck for you." So Duck came, and when I got there, he was a mess. I said. "What happened?" He told me he and Donnell, my brother, by the way, had been hanging out. And Donnell gave him a ride home. When he got out of the van, some guys started shooting. Donnell shot one of them. Diamond got shot in the hand.

It seemed that these guys were waiting on him. They had shot out his porch light and were laying in his yard in camouflage outfits. We drove by his house and the porch light was out and the house was dark. I took him to a motel and stayed that night with him. He was really upset. The next morning I called into work and spent the day with Diamond. Later that evening he took me home. Two nights later, he came about 1:30 a.m. and got me out of my mama's house. He told me to come on. I didn't understand why. He took me to the motel where he was staying. I asked him what was going on. He told me I didn't need to know. "Just go to bed." He asked me did I have to go to work, and I told him no.

When he started undressing, I noticed he had on a bulletproof vest. See when I started dating Diamond, he told me he had been shot seven times, so now it's eight. That evening when I was up on the streets, he told me to go get him a gun. He gave me the money and I bought him a .45. I figured he needed protection. That Christmas, I bought him a Derringer and my son bought me a pretty .25 automatic. It had a rose on the handle, black, trimmed in gold and it had a black and gold case. I loved that gun. It had special meaning.

Anyway, about three days later, Diamond came to get my car and left his car in my yard. Yeah, he was bad about coming to get my car. I think he liked being seen in my car. That way, I couldn't get a boyfriend!

I came back from Jamaica. I had bought my daughter's school clothes while I was there. This is about a couple of days later after I had come back. While I was over there by the way, I met this dread, redbone, light skinned man. He was a drug dealer. Seems like that's the only kind of men I attract. Anyway, Debra and I had got off the boat and were going shopping. The guy was standing on the corner. He was fine! Debra was my cabin roommate. I had got so drunk the night before, I couldn't find my cabin. I did find my sisters cabin. She couldn't have much fun because she brought her boyfriend with her. Ha!

The club was on the third floor of the boat. My cabin was on the second but for some reason, I ended up at her door. I knocked and told Linda I couldn't find my room. I had been balling out of control! She laughed at me and took me to my cabin. No, I ain't used to having a man wait on me. I worked the hell out of my cabin boy! I would find stupid reason's for him to do things for me. Bring me ice. My shoes need wiping, I got dust on them. Yeah right. I know he was glad to get rid of me!

On the dread, well, he asked us did we smoke weed. I told him "Yeah man." Then I asked him where the liquor store was. He said, "Right behind you, maaahn." Ha, ha. I love the way he talked. We went to the liquor store and the man who ran it was giving us all kind of different stuff to try. By the time Debra and I left, we were too through (drunk). He told us to go with him. We went to the restaurant, but we went on the top of it. They had tables and everything up there. We sat at a table and he rolled the longest joint I had ever seen. I was going to take it back to Diamond. Then he rolled another one and we smoked that one when we got through smoking the first one. The guy had given me his name and phone number. When we got back to the ship, I was feeling no pain. We had so much fun. We took a shower and got ready for dinner.

Now dinner was funny. We had to dress formal. I didn't know what to order, so I just ordered what the man sitting next to me ordered. He ordered a lobster dinner with a chocolate mousse for dessert. When dinner came, I am sitting there waiting on him to start eating because I had no idea how to even start eating that darn lobster. I had never eaten a lobster in my life! I mean I am a woman who came from a family of thirteen! Anyway, the man must have been watching me. I had the thing that you crack the lobster legs with open in my hand. I was just looking at it. So he said, "Excuse me miss, but you look lost." When he said it, he was smiling. I looked at him and smiled back and told him, "I am. Sir, I have no idea whatsoever how to open or crack, or whatever you are suppose to do. I only ordered this thing because you ordered yours." So he said, "Just watch and do what I do." I did, and it was really good. I enjoyed my meal, thanks to Mr. Edwards.

Now back to what I was talking about. Diamond came to get my car and left his car in the yard for me. I wasn't going anywhere that night. Linda called me on the phone. She told me to meet her at the police station. It seemed that Tarsha, Linda's daughter, had reported her car stolen. Her boyfriend, Lest, had stolen her car. Linda wanted me to meet her at the station. I went to ask my mama for her keys. She had a minivan. I loved to drive her van.

So on my way to the police station, which is right down the street from the club, Diamond and Leroy flagged me down. This was around 1:45 a.m. He asked me where I was going. I told him about Tarsha and Lest. He said, "Okay," and told me he would see me later. The next day when I saw him, he told me about Tammy. It seemed that Duck had gone in Tammy's house and killed her and shot the dog. He told the police that Diamond gave the order. Now I knew that was a lie. Diamond didn't tell him that. And he also told the police that he used my car.

Duck went in to kill Donnell, Tammy's son. But it was dark and Tammy was on the sofa. The dog barked and scared Duck and he shot Tammy and killed the dog.

Donnell had broken into Diamond's house a while back when I was living there. He went up on the streets, bragging about how he had broken in and stole ten thousand dollars, which was my son, Shon's money, and how he came in our bedroom while I was asleep and got the money out of the drawer. Now that pissed Diamond off. Hell, it pissed me off, too! So Duck calls himself showing his loyalty to Diamond and went there and killed that boy's mama. I still say Duck had been watching too much TV.

That's the second thing that went wrong. The first thing is Duck was jealous of Diamond and Shon's relationship. Also, Diamond had too much trust in Duck. Shon had told Diamond that Duck was going to be his downfall. He didn't pay Shon any attention. He had kicked Willie to the curb. He had even tried to set Willie up. I don't understand why he trusted Duck over everybody except me. No matter what, he knew I had his back. One thing about me, I am loyal.

Anyway, before that happened, Diamond told me he was going to buy a car. Well, while he was at the Jacksonville Airport, the police stopped him, checked all his bags and took his money, which was about $150,000. They gave him a receipt for it. That same night, Hattie calls me and asked me, "Where is Diamond?" I told her, "I didn't know. I don't live with Diamond." She told me, "Ok, well you two still talk don't you?" I said, "Yeah." Then she told me, "If he calls you, call me and let me know. He supposed to be coming down here to pick up his package." I told her, "Okay." About thirty minutes later, Diamond called to tell me what happened at the airport. I told him about Hattie's phone call. He had already talked to her. She asked him to send me down there. He said, "It's the weekend. Go down there and have some fun."

Something told me to tell him no. I wish I had. But I didn't. He asked me to come to his house the next day. So the next day, I went over to his house. He had a relative to take me to Jacksonville Airport where I caught a plane to Miami.

My cousin picked me up and took me to her house. On the way to her house, we stopped at a store and bought a six pack of Miller Light in the bottle and a bag of weed at one of her friend's houses. Then we went to her house. While we were there, she had me stand by her pool where she took pictures of me. Then she called Diamond and told him I made it. I stayed up late and talked to her son, Shawn.

Then I wanted to go to bed. She took me to the bedroom where I was going to be sleeping. She told me Diamond slept in that room when was there. She told me a lot of things I didn't know. She said, "Cuz, did you know I used to go shopping for you and the other girlfriend, Tamela?" I just looked at her and said, "What?" She said, "Yeah, Diamond always sent me to shop for him." She told me when he came there on business, she would take him shopping. She said, "I'm the one who hooked him up with his contact." I told Hattie, "I don't care about none of that. Where is his money he sent me to pick up? His package, he called it." She said, "I'll give it to you before you leave." So I told her, "Well, I'm going to bed." She said, "I've made your train reservation. You'll be leaving early in the morning."

When she left out of the room, I was kind of hurt. I mean damn, you're my daddy's first cousin and you helped my man cheat on me. I went to sleep thinking about that. The next morning, I got up and took a shower and got dressed. I put all my sleepwear and things in my travel bag. I took my curlers and make-up bag and went in the bathroom. Hattie knocked on the door and asked me what I want her to do with Diamond's package. I said, "Put it in the front of my bag. I don't need to go in that part of my bag." She said, "Okay." Then she said, "Cuz hurry up before you miss your train." I asked her, 'What's the rush if I miss it? I'll just catch another one." She said, "Girl, come on." So I told her, "Okay! I'm already coming." So I came out, put my stuff in the bag, got my purse and followed her out the door.

When we got to the train station, I should have known something was wrong. Listen at this. I went in to get my ticket and I said, "Do you have a ticket for Dianne Cooper?" He said, "No, but I have one for Dianne Johnson." I told him, "No, Johnson is my mama's maiden name. My name is Dianne Cooper." He said, "You sure?" I told him, "Yes, I'm sure." So he gave me a ticket. I left and went back to the car. When I got back in the car, I told Hattie, "Listen, that man told me he didn't have a ticket for Dianne Cooper. He had one for Dianne Johnson. What's up with that? That's madear's maiden name." She said, "Cuz I don't know. Anyway let's get you on the train." So I made it to the train. We gave each other a hug and I got on the train.

A bell should have went off in my head, but I was as they say, green to the game. I got my seat, then went to the dining car and got something to eat. I went to the bar and flirted with these white guys. After I went back to my seat, I sat there about thirty minutes looking out the window when the man said, "Jesup, GA." The train stopped so I got my bag and purse, and got off the train.

I thought Diamond would be there. But instead he sent Duck. He came toward me and said, "What's up, first lady?" He's the only one of Diamond's boys that call me that. I told him, "Nothing much. What's up and where is Diamond?" He said, "He's up on the streets. He told me to come get you and bring you up there." When we got to the car, Duck asked me, "You want to smoke a joint?" I said, "Sure." He said, "You got any papers?" I said, "Yeah in my purse." He popped the lock on the door and I got in. I was sitting on the passenger side looking through my purse for my rolling papers when somebody tapped on my window. I looked up and it was the police! I rolled my window down and he said, "Step out of the car please." I looked at

Duck and one was on his side of the car, too. So, I got out of the car, and so did Duck.

He told me who he was and asked me where I was coming from. I told him I had been to Miami to visit my cousin. Then I saw blue lights come on and it was more police. The one in front asked me what I did while I was there. I told him I hung out with my cousin and she took to me laundry mat and to the store. He asked me what I bought and I told him. Then he said, "Whose car is this?" I said, "Mine." He said, "May we search your car?" I said. "No you may not, and why do you want to search my car?" He said, "We have reason to believe you brought drugs back with you." I told him, "I don't have any damn drugs."

See I was still drunk, so I wasn't scared. He asked me, "Open the trunk please." I told him, "You open it." So the other officer told Duck to pop the trunk, and he did. When I took focus on the officer in front of me, and focused on my surroundings, man it was about ten cops plus three dogs! All I could think was what the hell! He asked me for my registration and insurance. I went to my glove compartment to get it. He went with me.

When I popped the glove compartment my gun was laying there. I reached for it and he jumped. I said, "Here you want it? It's legal. Here's the clip." I handed it to him along with the information he asked for. I looked over at Duck, and they were searching him. They got weed and a gun off him. I was mad when I saw that the gun they got off him was the Derringer I had bought Diamond for Christmas. How the hell he let Duck have something that I bought for him?

Anyway, the damn dogs were all in my car. And the cops were going through my bag. I heard one of them say, "Look'a here." I looked and he had a pair of jeans that looked like a size twenty. Mind you, I was a size five. When he unrolled them there was a brown paper bag inside. Inside the bag he pulled out a little plastic bag and put it in front of my face and said, "What is this?" I told him, "Look like baby powder to me." Then he pulled out another bag and said, "What is this?" I said, "Look like cookies to me." Then the other officer said, "We need to take some pictures." The one who had unrolled the jeans said, "We don't have any film." The first officer repeated, "We need to take some pictures of this." The second officer said, "Don't worry about it." Then he told me, "You can go." I said, "What?" He said, "You can go."

Duck and I got in the car and they took the dope and my guns and let us go. When we got in the car, I asked Duck, "What was that the cop held up in my face?" He said, "Crack and go crack. They call it butter." We went straight to the streets. Duck went and found Diamond while I went to the bar and ordered a beer! I sat on the bar stool and lit me a cigarette. Diamond came and stood in front of me and asked me what happened. I told him and after I finished, he said, "Okay. Duck said the same thing. I thought the nigger was lying, but since you said the same thing, I know he's telling the truth."

Then I said, "Baby those were Hattie's jeans and why did you send me to pick up dope?" He said, "I would never do that to you. When I tried a couple of weeks ago, they took my money from me at the airport. I wasn't going to send you. I was going to send Duck, but she asked for you." He said, "Don't worry about it. You ain't never been to jail before. The only thing they gone do if anything, is give you probation." That turned out to be a lie! He told me, "We'll talk later. Go on home. Everything is going to be alright."

During this time, Diamond was still not living in his house. I didn't see him for a couple of days. When I did see him, he told me he needed a favor. I said, "What?" He said, "I need five hundred dollars to go with what I got. My title to my car is in my brother's name. I need you to pawn your title. I will get it back for you." I told him, "Alright." So, Diamond, Duck and I went to pawn my title. A couple of days later on the weekend was when Duck went and killed Tammy. I met Diamond on the streets. He asked me had I heard about Tammy. I said, "Yeah. What the hell was Duck thinking?" Diamond said, "I don't know, he just better not put me in that shit." That same day, they arrested Duck for the murder of Tammy.

The next day, Diamond called and told me to pick up his clothes at the motel because he had been arrested for murder. Duck told the police that Diamond had ordered the hit. On my way down to the motel, cops came from everywhere. Vans and all cut me off and told me to get out of the car. They said, "Put your hands up and get out of the car." When I did, they had guns and rifles pointed at me. Then they said, "We're taking the car. Understand?" I said, "Yes." Then one cop came toward me and told me to get in the police car and asked me was there anyone I needed to call? I told him, "Yes. May I call my mama to come get me?" Then he told the other officer, "She's riding with me." When we got in the car he called my mama for me and told her where they were taking me.

Let me back up. After they had took the drugs and guns they let me go, then Diamond and I went to see his lawyer. Diamond's lawyer told us, they used me. They told Hattie to ask for me, because they didn't want me, they wanted Diamond. The police thought he would come and pick me up and they would catch him with the drugs, but since he sent Duck, that messed up their plans. But still, they let me go.

He told Diamond, "They thought if you didn't believe her, you would kill her." They were playing with my life. I was so mad. It turns out Hattie, my cousin, had got caught trafficking drugs a couple of weeks back. So she made a deal with them to help them catch Diamond. And she used me, her cousin, who has never done anything to her. After we left the lawyer's office, Diamond told me Hattie was jealous of me because she wanted him for herself. I asked him, "Why? Why not Tamela, your other woman?" He said, "She knows I only care about you." Now ain't that nothing? Now if Duck wouldn't have killed that woman, they might not have been so hard on us.

Anyway, back to me and the police. They took me in this little room and there was this lil detective who I couldn't stand, sitting there like we were the best of friends. I could not stand him! He said, "Hello Miss Cooper. My name is Detective John Taylor. I am not here to accuse you of anything. I want to ask you a few questions, alright?" I said, "Sure, alright." Then he said, "How long have you known Mr. Edmonds?" I told him, "About three years." Then he asked me, "Did he buy you that car?" I said, "I saved up for it. I do have a job and also I bought it with my income tax money." He said, "Oh yeah, okay. Do you know where Mr. Edmond gets his drugs from?" I told him, "No, I do not. He don't tell me his business." Then he said, "Whose drugs was that in your car?" I told him, "I guess Hattie's since she's the one who put them in my bag!" He looked at me and said, "You need to drop the attitude. You can go. I'll be talking to you." I said, "Whatever!" I got up to go, then he said, "I am trying to help you." I said, "Help me do what? I haven't done anything." He said, "Okay."

So I left out and my mama was sitting outside waiting on me. She said, "Baby, you in trouble?" I told her, "No madear, but they took my car." She said, "It'll be okay." We left out and went home. I hated worrying my mama. She was a good mother. She never put me down, no matter what I did. I loved her so much. When we got home, I went in and walked past my daughter's room. I went to the kitchen and got me a beer and sat in the living room looking at the TV, not paying much attention to it. I was thinking about all that had happened.

Diamond in jail for murder! And now they bring up this drug shit. The phone rang and I jumped. I answered, and it was Linda. She said, "Dianne what the hell's going on? Diamond's in jail and I just heard about you being taken down to the police station and they took your car!" I said to her, "Who told you that?" I just came home about ten minutes ago, and you know it don't take long. She said, "Somebody always see you. Anyway, what happened?" So I went through the story again. And she told me, "Baby sis, watch yourself. Something tells me, you are in some deep shit. I will be checking on you."

We said our goodbyes and then she hung up. Then Diamond called. I asked him how he was doing and he told me, "Baby they got me on the top floor by myself. I don't feel too safe. How you doing?" I told him how they had stopped me and had those guns on me. He said, "What the fuck they doing?" I told him about the detective. He said, "Watch him and be careful." Then I said, "I'll be by to see you tomorrow." He said, "What time?" I told him about 1:30. Then he said, "Okay." I told him, "See ya" and hung up.

I sat there thinking, what happened? This is crazy! I left out the living room and went to my bedroom and closed the door. Put some Keith Sweat on and rolled me a joint and laid on my bed feeling some type of way about Diamond and what he said about feeling safe. If I believed in the Lord, I would have prayed for myself and him, but since I didn't.... I got fucked up and fell asleep.

When I woke up, still dressed, the phone was ringing. It was

Jenny, my first cousin, calling being nosey. "Cuz girl, I heard about what's going on. Girl I can't believe Duck told those people that shit." I said, "Yeah, it's true. Look cuz, I got to go. I'll call you back okay? Bye." I hung up the phone, went through my clothes to find something to wear. I settled on a royal blue and black pant suit.

I ran a tub of water and took me a long bath. I always take the phone, a joint, cigarettes and a beer in the bathroom with me when I get in the tub. I didn't have to go to work because before all this mess happened, I had been in a car wreck. I was already mad at Diamond. It was the sixteenth of October, 1990. I was getting ready to go on vacation. I was working at Ware Manor Nursing home. I had gotten off from work and was driving down Oak Street and from nowhere a car came and hit the side of my car. I caught a glimpse of Diamond running towards my car and I was knocked out. I remember my head hitting the steering wheel.

When I came to, I was in the emergency room. The first person I saw was Diamond, then my mama, and my daughter, Juanita. They all looked scared to death. Man, they put me on crutches and I had a neck brace. I had to go to therapy. For my birthday, Diamond had bought me a new fall wardrobe. He came to check on me. I had my car fixed and while they were fixing my car, I had a rental. To be honest, I fell in love with the rental. I almost traded my car in but I couldn't do it because Diamond bought that car for me.

Anyway, after I got out of the tub, I got dressed and fixed me something to eat, which was a sandwich and I was eating it on my way out the door. I went to see Diamond. Man, he looked so bad. He looked stressed. He told me, "Don't worry about nothing. Everything is going to work out." I had to see his lawyer. I told him all that was going on and how they separated Diamond from everybody. He said he was going down there to see what was going on. After some time, I left the jail.

I went up on the block to see what was going on. I heard a lot of gossip about Diamond and how he had given Duck my car to go over Donnell's house just to scare him. But it was dark in the house and the dog barked and Tammy got up off the sofa and Duck just started shooting. I left from up there and went home. Time I got in the door good, mama said, "That detective called. He said for you to come back down there. He said he needed to talk to you." So I just turned around and went back down there.

As I was driving down there, I was thinking to myself, "What the hell does he want now? I've told this man I don't know anything about that man's business." When I got to the jail, I went to his office. He said, "Come in and sit down Miss Cooper. Can I get you something? Some coffee or soda?" I told him, "No thank you. What do you want with me?" He said, "I just want to ask you about Mr. Edmond. Have you been thinking about what I asked you the last time?" I told him, "Not really. Look, I don't live with the man and I am not his girlfriend at the moment. You should be asking his lady these questions, not me.

We're just friends." He said, "Yeah I know all about his so called girlfriend. But it seems he trust you more than he does her. And he seems to care more about you. You're the one he always calls. So, back to my question, are you going to help us and tell me who Mr. Edmond's contacts are and where he gets his drugs from? Also, what about the condo he has in California?"

I looked at that man like he had two heads. I tell you, I didn't have any understanding of what he was talking about and I told him that. But he thought I was lying and said, "Okay Miss Cooper you're not under arrest... yet." I just got up and left. I went to my sister Linda's house. I knocked on the door and she didn't answer. So I went to the backyard and she was on the phone. Shon and Leroy were there, too. I told her "Bitch get off the phone. I need to talk to you about some serious shit." Shon said, "Ma what's wrong?" Linda told whoever was on the phone that she had to call them back. Then she said, "Girl what's wrong with you?" I told her about the detective and what he said. I said, "Linda, he said I wasn't under arrest yet. He is going to lock me up. But damn, Linda I don't have anything to tell him. How's this man going to make me know something I don't know?"

Shon said, "Ma he just trying to scare you. You ain't never been to jail. He ain't gone do nothing. Don't worry about it." Leroy said, "Yeah right, he ain't got nothing on you." It's bad when you can't trust your own family. I said, "Damn. Man, I am tired of this man messing with me. He keep calling me talking about come down there and he be looking at me like I'm something good to eat." Linda laughed. "Yeah that's why he keeps calling you. He wants him a piece of chocolate." I looked at her and said, "Bullshit. I ain't the one." Leroy said, "Rat, don't go back down there by yourself." I said, "Alright. Damn, I am just tired of this shit. Hey, you think Diamond gone get out of this?"

Linda said, "I don't know. But I tell you what, I believe Duck is lying and I believe they gone hang Diamond's ass! They have wanted him a long time. And now that they got him in jail, they ain't about to let him out. Believe that." I said "Damn I feel so bad for him." Leroy said, "You need to feel bad for yourself. Stay away from the police, girl, I am telling you. They will use you to get Diamond. They know how he feels about you! Just pay attention." So I said, "Okay. Linda you got any beer?" She said, "No we done drunk it. Go over to the store and get a six pack, while I roll us a joint." Shon and Leroy said, "Well Auntie I'm gone. Ma, see you later." I told him "Okay baby."

Then I walked over to the store and got me and Linda a six pack. My mind was still on what that policeman said to me. When I came back, Linda was sitting in the living room. I got me a beer and handed her one. She was changing the channels on the TV. I said, "Linda, am I in trouble, tell the truth." She said, "Not if I can help it, you ain't. We gone get through this." So I hung out at her house. Then we started talking about Maureen and Gloria. Just about family. We got good and high. I left there when her man came.

I drove home feeling pretty good. Alexis was still up. When I came in the door she said, "Ma can I stay up with you?" I asked her, "Girl, why you ain't in the bed?" She said, "Mama I had to go to the bathroom. But now, can I stay up with you?" I had to laugh. My baby was so sweet at six. I told her, "Sure baby. Come on. Let's find something to watch on TV." She loves scary movies, and so did I. I found us a good one. We were enjoying our movie when the phone rings. It was the detective again. He said, "Miss Cooper, I need you to come see me." I said, "Man its 2:00 A.M." He said, "Yeah, but I need you to come see me." I said, "Sure, okay. Bye." I sat there thinking, something ain't right.

My baby and I slept on the sofa that night. That morning, the phone woke me up. It was Diamond. He said, "Hey baby how you doing?" I told him, "I'm glad you called, man. That damn detective called me at 2:00 a.m. telling me he wanted me to come down there. Baby, what the hell is going on?"

He said, "I think you need a vacation. Where do you want to go?" I said, "California, where my brother, Calvin lives." He said, "Okay, take off. When you get there, give Linda a number to give to me." I said, "Diamond, it's something you ain't telling me." He said, "It's a lot I wish I could tell you, Dianne. Just leave please." I told him, "Okay. I just got a check from my insurance for the car wreck." He said, "Go pick up some money from the house. You know where it is." I said, "Okay, talk to you later." So I called Linda and told her what

Diamond said. She said, "Girl we got to get you away from here. Where is madear?" I said, "In her room." Linda said, "Put madear on the phone and go get the money and start packing your shit."

So I went over to the house and looked in the mailbox and got the envelope out. It had a couple of thousand in it. I went back home and Linda was there. My mama looked so worried. She had called Gloria and told her I was coming. So they took me to Jacksonville to Gloria's house and went back home. Alexis looked at me like she knew something was wrong. I hated leaving my kids. Everything was happening so fast, I couldn't think. I told my baby, "I'll be back for you." She didn't say anything. I wanted to cry! My mama and Linda hugged me and they left and went back to Waycross. Gloria asked me what I wanted to do. I told her, "I know I ain't going to see that detective again." She said, "I'm calling cousin Roscoe. He'll know what to do."

Chapter 5

So Gloria called cousin Roscoe and he came over. He told me to come and go with him. He told Gloria, "I'm going to take her to my house. I'll handle it from here." I hugged my sister and left. While Roscoe and I were in his van, he asked me to tell him what happened. So I told him about Diamond and Duck, and how I was on the train and Hattie had put dope in my bag. When I got to the part where they let me go, he said, "They let you go?" I said, "Yeah!" He told me, "You know they were hoping Diamond would hurt you or better yet, kill you. You do know that?" I said, "To be real with you, I never thought about it. But yeah, I'm sure they would have loved that, but it didn't work out like that. Diamond took my word for it." He said, "Lucky you."

So we got to the house and he got my bags out of the van and opened the door and I went in the house. It brought back memories of the last time I was at this house. It was when I had got mad at my daddy and took my kids. During that time, I only had Shon and Nita. My daddy had told me to get out the house. He didn't think I would leave, but I did. My mama gave him so much hell, he came to

Jacksonville to ask me to come back home. I sure do miss that man.

Anyway, Roscoe told me to make myself at home while he checked the bus station out to buy me a ticket for California tomorrow. So I went and took me a bath and got comfortable. I was watching TV when Roscoe came back. He had went to the liquor store and asked if I wanted something to drink. He said, "I'm sure you do. Dianne, I can't believe this is happening." I lit me a Salem and told him, "Me either." I said, "Roscoe, I should be scared, but I ain't. Why is that?" He said, "The hell if I know, but I do know I am scared enough for both of us. Cuz, you are in some deep shit. How deep, I don't know. We got to get you away in the morning." I told him, "Good night." I sat there, got loaded and watched TV. I couldn't tell you what was on it. I just sat and drank and smoked, looking crazy. I finished my cigarette and curled up on the sofa and went to sleep. Roscoe woke me up and asked if I wanted something to eat. I told him, "No thanks." I got up, took a bath, got dressed and told him I was ready.

They had called Calvin to tell him I was coming. So he took me to the bus station. Roscoe waited until I got on the bus. I sat there and I had no idea that I would never see my cousin again after that. See, he died since I was locked up. Anyway, I had four long days to travel on that bus before I got to Sacramento, CA. I mean, that was four LONG days. I fell off to sleep and when I woke up this man was sitting next to me feeling my thighs. I looked at him and he was smiling at me. I got my ass up and moved. I went and sat between two old people in the very back of the bus by the bathroom. Now that man scared me, so I was kind of scared to go to sleep until he got off. When we would stop, I would stand by the bus and smoke. Other times I would go and get me a burger and a coke.

At last, I made it to Sacramento. When I got off the bus, I looked around and went to the phone to call my brother. I couldn't get him. I got in one of the taxi's that were lined up at the bus station and gave him Linkie's address. We rode and the meter was ticking. I didn't want the man to think I didn't know where I was going because I was sure he would go the long way around. So I said to him, "You do know where Communion Commons is, don't you?" He said, "Where are you from?" I said, "What does that have to do with the question?" He said, "I can tell you're not from here by the way you talk, and yes I know where that is, to answer your question." I didn't say anything else. I just enjoyed the ride. And he did take the long way around because that ride cost me forty one dollars. That's the price I paid for opening my country ass mouth! And he put me out at the wrong apartment.

I got out of the taxi and went to knock on the door. I knocked and this woman comes to the door. Mind you, I've never seen Linkie so I don't know what she looks like. When she came to the door, I said "Hi. I am looking for Linkie Moore." She said "She don't live here. Who are you?" I told her, "I'm her boyfriend, Calvin's sister from

Georgia." She said, "Oh well, Linkie lives down that way." She pointed at apartment 34. I said, "Thank you." I picked up my bag and started walking where she pointed. It seems Calvin was living in the projects. I walked straight to the apartment, and as I got to Linkie's door, she was coming out. I said to her, "Excuse me but I am looking for Linkie." She said, "Who are you?" I said, "I'm Dianne, Calvin Cooper's sister." That's when she broke out in a smile and said, "I'm Linkie. Let me help you with your bags."

When I walked in her apartment, the first thing I noticed is she didn't have a back door. I was walking behind her and I said, "Linkie, why your apartment don't have a back door?" She said, "None of the apartments have back doors." I told her, "In Georgia all apartments have back doors. Shit, if the police drove up in here, you only have one way in and one way out. I'm not too crazy about that." She said, "The police don't have any reason to come up in here, so chill sister-in-law. Calvin should be getting off from work after while." I said, "Look, I am going to take a shower and change clothes, and then we can talk. Also, I need to use your phone. Don't trip, I'll pay for all my calls, or I will call collect, alright." She said, "Sure."

I sat my bags down and opened them to see what I was going to change into. I found a pair of black flats, a small top and a pair of walking shorts. I got my curlers out and plugged them up. I went into the bathroom and I didn't see a closet with towels and washcloths in it, so I yelled out the bathroom door to Linkie to ask her, "Where do you keep your extra washcloths and towels?" She said, "I got some in my room. I'll bring them to you." And she did. I told her "Thank you." I cut the water on and got the right temperature, got in and was standing under the water thinking where do I go from here?

Lord, I can't believe I am here in Sacramento, California. How am I going to get my baby here? Maybe I could get Linda to bring her to me. Nita graduates this year from high school so it won't be a problem to get her here. Maybe she can bring Alexis to me. Lord, help me! What am I going to do now? All of this was going through my mind as I stood in that shower. I just started crying. I was so sick of my life at that moment. I started talking to myself, "Shut up Dianne. Crying is not going to help you."

I finished my shower, got out the bathroom, and went in the kitchen where I had the curlers plugged up and bumped my hair. I went in the bathroom again and put on my makeup. As I was coming out the bathroom, I heard somebody calling Linkie. I knew that voice anywhere. It was my brother, Calvin. I ran out the door, he hugged me and said, "Well I be damned, Dianne baby. I can't believe it." I asked him, "I called your job. Where were you and why weren't you at the bus station to pick me up?" He said, "Girl, my car wouldn't start. I'm glad you made it. So are you hungry or what? I'm going to fix you something I bet you never had." I said, "What?" He said, "You ever had African spaghetti?" I said, "African spaghetti, what's in it?" He said, "You'll see. Come on and go to the store with me."

We went back to his car and he had some men in the car. He said, "Hey y'all, this is my sister, Dianne. Dianne these are my boys, Clarence, Tim and John." I said, "Hey, how y'all doing?" They started laughing, "Hey man, where's your sister from?" He said, "Georgia, why?" They said, "I like the way she talks, man. Damn your sister sounds country." They started laughing again. I told them, "I'm glad you find me funny. I am not here to entertain you!" Calvin said, "Hey nigger, lay off my sister."

We were driving down the road. I was looking out the window enjoying the sights. It was so different from what I was used to. Calvin said, "Look Dianne, later on tonight we're going to the club. We won't leave until about 12:30 a.m., so we have lots of time to hang out." Calvin said, "Do you still drink Miller in the bottle?" I said, "Yea". Then Clarence said, "Hey, I want you to try some of this." He had some Seagram Seven and chocolate milk. I said, "What the hell is that?" He said, "Wait 'til we get back to the house, you gonna like this." We finished our shopping and went back to the apartment. Calvin said, "Alright, let's get some weed. Who got some money?" Nobody said anything. He told his friends, "Man come on, shit. Chip in. I ain't buying everything." I told him, "Calvin I'll chip in." He said, "Cool, what about you niggers?" We got the money together. I gave him a twenty. He called Linkie out the room and said, "Linkie, you and Dianne go get the weed." I said, "How far we got to go?" Linkie said, "Come on. It's just through the alley."

We left out and walked across the pavement and down through the alley. It was some little apartment through there. We got some green bud and went back to the apartment. When we got back, I went and got me a beer and popped the top. It tasted good going down. I tell you, I needed that. I felt so out of place. It had gotten dark and Clarence said, "Hey y'all, it's hot in here. Let's go outside." We went outside and sat on top of the car. It seemed like a lot of cars were in the parking lot. The music was playing. It seemed like the party was outside.

We went over to all the cars and it seemed like everybody knew Linkie. They went to hollering, "Hey Linkie Moore, what's up, and who you got there?" She said, "Hey what's up. This is my sister-in law, Dianne. She's from Georgia." They all said hey and they were telling me their names. Clarence, with his smart red ass said, "Hey man, she talks funny. She sound so damn country. I love to hear her talk." I told him, "Man what I tell you about that shit? I ain't here to entertain you. Get off me, will ya." Then he burst out laughing and the way he sounded, I started laughing too, and then everyone started laughing. Then he said, "Hey country, I am not picking on you. I like you. You're a little spitfire." I said, "Hey, that's not my name." Then this girl Wanda said, "That fits you, no disrespect. That's going to be our nickname for you." I said, "What the hell." Clarence said, "Now that you're not going to shoot any of us this is what I wanted you to try."

He put the chocolate milk in the liquor and started shaking it up and then pulled some cups out the bag. He said, "Here spitfire, try this." He poured me some in the cup. When I tell you that stuff was good! I told him, "Not bad," and I also said, "Look, is my name country or spitfire?" He said, "Both because you're both. You're a little country ass girl that talks a lot of shit." My brother thought that was just so funny. He said, "Damn man, you sure know my sister, and if you ain't sharp, she will shoot your ass for real." We had fun that night. We stayed out there in the parking lot until about 11:30 p.m., and then everybody left to go regroup for the club.

We went to Fresno that night. I went and took a much needed shower. I was so damn high or drunk. I didn't know which, but whatever one it was, I came down only to get back up there on the way to Fresno. We were smoking and drinking. It was two car loads of us. Half of them I don't even remember their names, which as far as I am concerned is a good thing. When we got to the club, boy I tell you, these people were sharp! I mean the clothes. They truly knew how to dress. Of course, I was no joke myself. A lot of them asked me where I got my outfit. As I learned from Hattie, all my clothes came from Miami, FL. I had on a black and gold dress and gold pumps with three inch heels. I danced all night long. I must say, I had a lot of fun. We balled out of control. We left about 5:30 a.m. I was tired. I wasn't used to this kind of party, but guess what? It didn't take long! We would sleep all day and party all night.

Now the next day, which was Saturday, I woke up about one in the afternoon. I slept on the sofa, by the way. I got me some clothes out of my bag, then went and showered. Linkie told me we were going to do laundry, which is what I needed to do. So I got myself together and helped her get the kids. Yes, she had three kids, two girls and one boy. We all lived in that two bedroom apartment. On my way out the door with the clothes and detergent in my hand, a police car pulled up. My heart dropped to my stomach. I still haven't called home yet? I went and put the clothes in the car. I was coming back from the car while Linkie was talking to the cop. She said, "Come here, sister-in-law." I said, "Shit," and went over to the car. He was smoking a cigarette and leaning halfway out the car. Linkie said, "This is Darrell. Darrell, this is Calvin's sister, Dianne."

He asked me, "How long are you planning on being in our lil city?" I said, "I don't know yet." He said, "Well if you decide to stay, I would like to take you and show you around, unless you have something against cops." I said, "No, not at all. Well I got to go, I need to use the phone. Nice meeting you." I got away from that car. I left him and Linkie talking. I went and sat down on the sofa. I was so outdone. I couldn't believe she had done that. I picked up the phone and called home. My mama answered the phone. "Baby how you doing? I am so glad you called." I said, "I'm alright madear. What's going on?" She said, "Shon's in jail and the police came here looking for you. They said, you can come back and get your car."

I said, "Wait a minute, Shon's in jail? For what?" She said, "For drugs and they said he got to go to boot camp for ninety days. He said when you call not to worry about him. He'll be okay. And Diamond called. He said for you to call home at 9:00 and you'll do a three way. He said call Linda's house." I said, "Madear, I know you worried, but don't please. I am okay. Calvin and I are doing fine. How are the girls?" She said, "Missing you. Nita said when she graduates, she will be coming there." I asked her, "When is it?" She said, "Next Friday." My heart broke. I knew I had to be there. I asked her where they were? She said they were over to their daddy's house, but would be back tomorrow. I told her, "I'll call over there." Then I said, "Madear I love you." She said, "I love you too, baby. Stay safe." I said, "I will, bye." She said, "Bye."

I was getting ready to call over to Rev. Cooper's house when Linkie hollered, "Dianne come on, let's finish these clothes." I said, "Alright, I'm coming." I came out the door with my purse on my shoulder. I got in the car. I said, "Where's Calvin?" She said, "Gone with his friends somewhere." We went to the laundry mat. While we were doing our laundry, Linkie said, "Dianne, Calvin told me a little about what was going on with you. So what happened? Why did you come here?" I was pissed with Calvin for telling my business. I didn't know what to tell her. I mean, I don't know this woman. Linkie was a tall woman about five nine. She wore a weave. She had a very tacky weave job. I had no understanding of my brother's choice in women. I mean, he had a wife worth 2.3 million and here he was living in the projects in a two bedroom apartment with a woman on welfare who has three kids. I just didn't understand.

Anyway, I told Linkie that my boyfriend was in jail for a murder he didn't have anything to with and they kept questioning me and to keep me out of it, he sent me on a vacation. She looked at me and said, "Girl I am so sorry. That's why you got away from Darrell. Girl, what are you going to do? You think they will come get you?" I didn't say anything. Then she said, "Dianne, you didn't have anything to with it for real, did you?" I said "No girl." She said, "Well you know Calvin said you had some money and you wouldn't mind helping out with stuff. All of us have to eat." I said, "That's what my brother said. I've been giving him money since I been here." Then I said, "I think I need to find me somewhere else to go." She said, "No, you ain't got to do that, we can all stay together." I said, "Look, if I am a problem, let me know and I can leave." She said, "No girl, we're family. Don't worry about it. Let's just get this laundry done and go out to the park before it gets dark." "Alright," I told her. But what I was thinking was, I can't believe this! My own brother is turning on me, now what? I can't sleep on this woman's sofa forever. What am I going to do? Some of the clothes were dry so I got them out and started folding them.

When we had finished, we put the clothes in the trunk and she took me to the park. I didn't talk and she didn't either. I sat there, cigarette in hand, looking out the window. We arrived at the park. I got out of the car and I was just looking around. It was beautiful! It had a pond with ducks in it. All the lil kids running and playing made me think about my baby. Damn, I miss my kids. I heard somebody call Linkie. She went over to the car. Three men were standing, more like leaning on a car. I was still propped on Calvin's car, checking out my surrounding and feeling sorry for myself. I looked toward Linkie and she and one of the men were walking toward me. When she got close enough to me, she said, "Sister-in-law, I want you to meet a friend of mine. Michael, meet Dianne Cooper. She's from Georgia. She's my old man's sister." He said, "Hi Dianne." I said, "Hi Michael." I was checking him out. Nice, I thought to myself.

Chapter 6

Mike asked me did I have any kids. I answered, "Yes, three. What about you?" He said, "One." I watched Linkie walk off and I knew she was trying to hook me up with this man. Not that I was mad or anything. Hey, Mike was fine. He was about five eight, he wasn't all black, but he was mixed with something. He looked more Indian. He had nice black, straight hair. He had it back in a ponytail. He's the reason I have a thing for men with ponytails today.

He said, "How old are your children?"

"Six, eighteen and nineteen."

"Are you planning to move here?"

I told him "I don't know, I'm thinking about it." He looked at me and tilted his head and asked if he could call me. I said, "Sure, but I don't know Linkie's telephone number by heart." He laughed and said, "That's okay, I already have it." One of his friends said, "Hey Mike, we're leaving." He said, "Hold up, I'm coming." He told me, "I'll be talking to you." I said, "See you." Linkie came back to the car smiling and talking about, "My friend Mike likes the Georgia peach." I said, "Why did you do that girl? You're crazy, but he is fine. What is he mixed with?" She told me Mike was black and Indian and French. I said, "Damn, no wonder he's so fine." She said "He told me that you were cute." I said, "For real?" She said, "Yea. Look we ain't got long, so let's walk around the park and then we're going to have to go."

We took us a stroll around the park. It was really nice. Linkie knew a lot of people. She introduced me to a lot of guys. I didn't care for them. Most of them were drug dealers. She told me a little about Michael. She told me that Mike's brother is a doctor and his sister-in-law is a lawyer secretary. Mike works at the hospital. He has one child, a little girl. He was crazy about the child's mother. But the little girl's mother dogs him big time. She said, "Mike's the type that don't hit women, so she takes advantage of that. You and Mike are going to get along fine. He loves to drink beer too, but you guys drink different brands. You're the Miller by the bottle and he's the Saint Ives by the quart kind of guy."

We made our rounds and headed back to the car. I got in and we headed back to the apartment. When we got there Linkie's little girl said, "Aunt Dianne, your mama called." I said, "Thanks sweetie. Have you seen Calvin?" She said, "No, he hasn't come home yet." So I helped Linkie separate the clothes and put them up. Then I told her, "Look, I need to go to the store. Do you need anything?" She said, "Yea, bring back some beer." I told her I would, but first I had to change out of these clothes.

I put on a pair of blue dress pants, a blue and black top and some black flats. I headed out for the store with my purse slinging on my shoulder. The store was about four blocks from the apartments. This was my first time going by myself. On my way, I saw this black car. At first, I thought it was my imagination so I kept walking, and then when I turned the corner a few minutes later, I saw the car again. Then it hit me, that car was following me. "It's got to be the police," I said to myself. I just kept walking. I reached in my purse and got me a cigarette, lit it and kept walking. I got to the store, bought my beer and cigarettes, paid for them and left. I went out the door and was headed back to the apartment when I saw these guys. They all had on red bandanas.

One of them said, "Hey you, where the hell you think you're going with that blue shit on?" I told him, "I am going to mind my damn business and who the fuck is you to question me? Nigger you don't know nothing about me." He came up and said, "Where you from?" I got a little scared. I saw this man was not playing with me. I told him I was from Georgia and I was living in Communion Commons at the moment with my brother's girlfriend, Linkie. He said, "Linkie Moore?" I said, "Yeah, you know her?"

"Yeah, I know her. Look, let me explain things to you. I don't understand why Linkie didn't tell you not to wear that damn color in this neighborhood, alright? This is blood territory. You have on the wrong shit. You could have gotten beat down, but you're so damn cute and I kind of like the way you talk. You a little gangster bitch ain't you?"

Man, when he called me a bitch, I forgot about being scared. I said, "Motherfucker, I got your damn bitch. Who the hell you calling a bitch?" He looked at me like he was going to knock my head off. Then he burst out laughing. He told me, "I like you, you alright." He told the other boys, "Look, when you all see her around here, don't fuck with her alright?" He turned back to me and said, "What's your name, Georgia peach?" I said, "Dianne." He said, "Dianne, my name is Tony. Nice meeting you. Come on, let me walk you back to Linkie's. I'm going to try to keep you from getting in trouble between here and there." I'm five feet six, so Tony was about five feet seven and a half. He had a bad boy look about him. One diamond in his ear, dark skinned, long braids in his head, one gold tooth in the front and very bow legged. He had a nice smile.

Tony and I became quick friends before we made it to the apartments. When we hit the corner Linkie and Calvin was sitting outside in front of the apartment. Linkie said, "I thought I might have to come find you." Then she said, "What's up Tony?" Tony said "Linkie, why didn't you tell her about the dress code around here? What were you doing, trying to get her killed?" Linkie said, "Oh shit man, sister-in-law I wasn't thinking." Then she turned to Calvin and said, "You should have told her, she's your sister." Calvin said, "Yeah I should have. Sorry sis. I wasn't thinking." Tony just shook his head. "Well she's alright. Nobody's going to fuck with her. Well Dianne, you give me a beer and I'll fire up a joint. What you say?"

"No problem," I said and he laughed. He said "I love that Georgia accent." I looked at him and said, "Man, am I the only person from Georgia you people have ever heard talk?" They said, "Your brother, but he's been here so long that he's lost his accent. Boo, you is fresh meat." I told him, "You are a very sick man." He just smiled. We sat outside and kicked it for a while, then all the cars started gathering in the parking lot. We all walked over there. While I was over there, I remembered I needed to call home, so I told them that would be right back.

I ran over to the apartment. Just as I was walking in the door, the phone rang. It was my mama. I said, "Hello?" She said, Baby, that's you?" "Yes ma'am," I said. She said, "The police came here looking for you. Alexis was in the yard and they asked her was you her mama. She told them yes. Then they asked her do you know where your mama is? Alexis is one smart little girl, she told them, 'I ain't going to tell you where my mama is so you can put her in jail like you did my brother. Get out of my yard.' Then she came and told me, 'The police want my mama, madear.'"

Then she said, "Before I could ask the question, the police were knocking on the door. They said, 'Are you Dianne Cooper's mother?' I said yes. He said, 'My name is Detective Taylor and this is Detective Adams. We're looking for your daughter. Do you know where she is?' I said 'No I don't'. Then he asked me when was the last time I saw you. I said, 'What do you want with my daughter?' He said, 'Miss Cooper, your daughter has been indicted and wherever she is, she needs to come back. When you talk to her, tell her she can get her car back."

I asked my mama, "What's indicted?"

She said, "I asked him and he told it means you could go to jail for a very long time." I asked her, "What did you say?" She said, "I told him, if I see or talk to her, I'll tell her. He just looked at me and said, 'Do that Ms. Cooper.'

I said to my mama, "Oh man, I can't come home now." She said, "Don't come back right now anyway. Everything will work out baby." Then she told me to call Linda. I told her I would. Then I asked her where was Nita. She told me she was over to Linda's house. I told her, I loved her and to put Alexis on the phone. Alexis got on the phone. "Mama?"

"Yes baby,"

"Mama, is the police going to get you?"

"I hope not baby, because I plan on getting us an apartment and get a job, so I can take care of you."

She said, "Is Nita coming too?" I told her, "Sure Nita's coming. She's my baby too!"

Alexis said, "Why do Nita have to come? She's big. She can take care of herself. I am little." I said, "Now Alexis, that's your sister and I am her mama too. I miss you and I miss her."

"Okay then" she said. "If she has to, I guess she can come.

When you coming mama?"

"I'll let you know, okay? Until I do come, be good and do what madear tell you to do."

"What about Nita? Does she have to do what Madear says?" I said, "Yes she does."

"Okay then, mama." I told my baby, "Mama got to go. I love you. Always remember I love you, okay?"

"Okay mama. I Love you too."

I had no understanding of what to do. I knew I couldn't just stay here. I needed help! I got myself together and went back outside. I couldn't just lie down and go to bed because I slept on the sofa in the living room. I was headed back out the door and the phone rang. I picked it up and it was Linda. She said, "Hi baby sis, how you holding up?" I told her, "Calvin is living with this girl. This is not his apartment. I got to find me somewhere to go. All they want to do is spend my money partying. If I knew he was living like this Linda, I wouldn't have come here." She said, "Calm down. Now listen, Diamond is on the other end and he wants to talk to you. I'm going to click over and let you guys talk some more." I told her, "Okay."

Then I heard, "Dianne?"

"Yeah," I said. "What's going on, baby? How are you doing and what are they saying?" He said, "Baby, I don't think I'm going to beat this one. That damn Duck keep lying on me and telling them people I told him to do that. I didn't tell him that. Do you believe me?"

"Diamond of course I believe you. Look baby, these people said I was indicted. They have been to my mama's house and everything, man. I need to get my kids. How am I going to take care of my kids? I can't leave my kids in Georgia while I am in California."

He said, "I don't know, Dianne. I can't do anything right now. They got me here by myself. It's so much I need to tell you. Look, don't come back here. I know you want Alexis and Nita, but if you come back here, you won't be doing them any good because they are going to lock you up. Look I'm sorry things worked out like this. I'm going to figure out something. I got to go. Love you."

I said, "Love you too, baby." Linda finally picked up the phone. "Dianne?" I said, "Yeah." She said, "Please take care of yourself. Look, graduation is next week. We're going to do all we can to make sure Juanita is represented like what she's used to. So call us okay, baby sis?" I told her, "Okay." She said, "Love ya." I told her, "I love you too." I hung up the phone and went back outside. I crossed over the parking lot.

Calvin said, "Damn, girl. You been on the phone that whole time?" I said, "Yeah, I had to check on my kids if that's alright with you." Then Donna said, "Hey Georgia peach, is that cross on that chain real?" I said, "Yeah, it's real. Why?" She said "Girl, you can't be wearing stuff like that around here. You going to lose your fingers with that rock on it. Where do you think you're at?" I told her, "I never thought about that." She said, "Want to sell it?" I said, "I might as well. I can't wear it." She said, "I'll buy the chain and the rock on your finger for five hundred." I said, "What the hell?" Donna said, "I'll be back tomorrow night and bring you your money." I told her, "And you'll get it tomorrow when you bring me my money." She said, "Do all Georgia women have attitudes like you?" I told her, "I wouldn't know. I don't know every woman in the state of Georgia." She laughed and said, "Got to go. See you tomorrow night, Ms. Attitude." I said, "Yeah. See ya!" She had a nice truck. She and her clique left.

Tony had come while I was gone. He said, "What's up girlfriend. Gotcha a beer and a joint. Damn, you look like you can use it, too. What's up with you?" I told him it was personal. I asked him how things were going with him. He said, "Oh no problems. I'm a little pissed off, but we'll get them back." I said, "What are you talking about?" He said, "Those motherfuckers almost blew my boy's head off last night." I said, "Who?" He said, "The tall one that was with me the other day when you came out the store." I said, "Oh yeah. I never did know his name. Oh man, not him." He said, "Yeah. He was walking to his car and they just opened fire on him. He should have known better to even be over in that neighborhood for one, and at that time of night fucking with that stinking whore. Now he's dead and that bitch will be gone on to the next nigger. I should go and blow her ass up."

I said, "Don't do that. It's not like she did it. Like you said, he knew better. I'm sorry about your friend, seriously." He said, "Thank you. Look, I got to pull out. Watch yourself." I told him, "You too." It started thinning out.

I went back in the house. It was almost one in the morning. By now, I had just laid down on the sofa and slowly fell asleep. I woke up to a house full of people. I sat up and looked around me. I looked at the TV and it was a basketball game on, the Lakers. Calvin and his crew were sitting at the bar and Linkie was in the living room. I counted eight, including Linkie. I got up and went in the kid's room and went through my bag, grabbed my clothes, a towel and a wash cloth and went to the shower. I got it together, dressed, bumped my hair and came out. I went and got my cigarettes out of my purse and when I stepped back in the living room, I saw Michael. He had a quart of Saint Ives in his hand, talking to Linkie. He looked at me and smiled. He said, "Well hello lady." I said "Well hello yourself. How's it going?" He said, "So so. Hey, want to go for a ride with me?" I said, "Love to."

I was looking around thinking, man how can she live like this? I told Linkie, "See you later." She was standing by Calvin and he said something to her. She said, "Oh Dianne, I need to talk to you please." I told Mike to go ahead, I'm coming. I asked Linkie, "What's going on?" She told me her brother was getting out of prison and was coming to live with her, "But don't trip. He can sleep on the floor." I said, "What?"

"He ain't gonna be here long. You can still sleep on the sofa. Look, the phone bill came this morning." I said, "Yeah, how much are my calls?" She said, "Sixty two dollars, but look, could you help out with the light bill? Just pay your part of the phone bill and give me a hundred dollars on the lights." "Yea," I said. "No problem." I gave the money to her and Calvin said, "Hey sis got ten dollars on a bag?" I said, "I'm about to jet with Mike, but here." I gave him the ten. He took it with a smile and said, "I'll give it back." "Yeah right," I said. He laughed and said, "For real, girl." I just walked out the door. Mike was leaning against the car when I came out. He said, "You are catching hell here, ain't you?" I said, "How you guess?" He told me, "It's not hard. I know Linkie and your brother is not here much. Seems like to me he would have tried to help you find somewhere to go. Come on." I said, "Where are we going?" He said, "Where I first spotted you, pretty lady. To the park." He opened the door for me and I got in the car.

We rode and he pointed different places out to me. We went to the park and we talked about everything and nothing. That night he took me to his brother's house. It was late, so I went in the den and we watched a movie. Then he told me he was tired and he was going to bed. He brought me a big t-shirt, a blanket and a pillow. I slept in the den and got me the first good night's sleep in about a month. The next morning, Mike had a towel, washcloth and soap lying on the table. I went and took a shower and when I came out, he was fixing breakfast. I asked him where everybody was. He said they were over his mother's.

He said he told his mama about me and he didn't want to wake me up, so he stayed behind. I told him, "Oh man, I feel bad about that."

He said, "Oh, it's okay. You look like you needed some good sleep. You also seem like you need a friend. What's going on with you and why are you living in that hellhole? It don't fit. I can tell by the way you dress and the lost look you seem to have on your face. I know you don't know me, but you need a friend."

I felt like crying. I just dropped my head and said, "Can I eat first? I haven't had a real meal in awhile. I've been living off of junk food." He said, "Alright, let's eat and then you tell me what's going on." So we sat and ate, then I helped him clean up the kitchen. I asked him how long had he been living with his brother. He said, "A couple of months. I was living with my little girl's mama, but we broke up. I let her keep the apartment and everything in it. I was getting ready to ask her to marry me until I found out she was cheating on me. I couldn't believe it, but hey I guess she wasn't for me. I did love her very much. You always hear women saying all they need is a good man. Then they cheat on them. Why do women do that? I would have done about anything for her and she did that to me. The worst part was she didn't care when I asked her about it all. She said, 'I hated for it to end like this, but I was going to tell you.' I just moved out. But I couldn't put my baby out."

I told him, "A lot of women are looking for a good man. Just because one cheated it don't mean all of us do."

"Alright, I guess I got a defective model." I told him, "More like stupid." We both laughed. Mike said, "Alright, spill it. What's up?" I took a sip of orange juice and told him about the police coming to my mama's house and about Diamond. When I finished he said, "Damn girl, and you been walking around with that and nobody to help you? Damn! I am so sorry and I'm complaining about my girl cheating. That's funny compared to what's going on with you. Look, lets' go over to Linkie's so you can change clothes and let's see if we can make something happen."

Mike and I spent most of all our time together after that. We became good friends. I used to love to braid his hair for him. He used to love to dance. His brother used to have a lot of cookouts, and when they did I would stay over. I just about lived there. Linkie's brother had come and was sleeping on the floor. I had gotten to where I hated to go over there. About a month after Mike and I had become friends, we became lovers.

Sometimes when I was over at Linkie's, Diamond would call and Mike would be over there. I would be braiding his hair while talking to Diamond. He would look up at me when I would tell Diamond I loved him. Hey, it wasn't a lie! I did love him. In a way, I still do. He's a special kind of man. I hope to see Diamond again one day. Just to talk to him. Anyway, Mike knew when it came to Diamond everything was on hold. I was worried about Diamond. Mike took me to this place and got me some food stamps and they paid for me to live in this motel. So that was my home off and on. Linkie's brother moved out and it seems, so did my brother. I stayed half with Linkie and half in the motel. I gave Linkie the stamps. I really didn't need them.

Mike and I decided we were going to get an apartment and he was going to Georgia to get my girls for me. The night Juanita graduated from high school, I was told when they called her name, my sisters took pictures and said, "This is for your mama." They told me the police were everywhere. They thought I would show up, and I almost did. But my mama had told me not to come back, so I didn't. I cried hard that night. I couldn't stand it.

About four months later, Mike and I had gone to this motel to spend the weekend together. We had just finished making love and he had gone to get something to eat. I was sitting up, smoking a joint when I looked out the window there were policemen everywhere. Then there was a knock on the door. They said, "POLICE, open up." I got up, put on my clothes and went to the door. When I opened the door they said, "Are you Dianne Cooper from Waycross, Georgia?" I said, "Yes, I am." He said, "Do you know Eugene Edmond?" I answered, "Yes." He said, "I have a Governor's Warrant for your arrest. If I was you I would sing like Al Green." I said, "Well since I'm going to be gone for a while, I have a couple of beers and a joint. Do you mind if I just go ahead and knock them out?" He said, "No, go ahead."

So I went and put my shoes on and got my purse and then I sat on the bed and lit my joint while he asked me questions that I had no answers to. When I finished, I was feeling no pain. The black guy driving the jeep said to the white guy, "She's riding with me." So I half walked to the jeep and propped my feet up on the dash board. I told him, "Turn your music on." He did and that song, Been Around the World and I Can't Find My Baby was on. He said, "Hey do you understand how much trouble you are in? You had to do some real shit for them to come at you like that. What did you do?" I said, "Mister, I didn't do a damn thing. The people think I know stuff that I truly don't know."

He said, "Well if I were you, I would make some shit up, because these folks in Georgia want your pretty little ass real bad." I said, "Well now they got me." He said, "It's sad. I wish I would have ran into you sooner." When he said that, we were pulling into the Sacramento County Jail parking lot. He drove around to the back, put cuffs on and took me in. When I walked in, I was read my rights. Finger printed. Took my clothes and put me in a damn orange jumpsuit. They told me I had one phone call. I called my mama and these are the words I told her: "Madear, they caught me and I'm in the Sacramento County Jail and I'm glad because, madear I am tired."

She said, "Well baby, are you alright?" I said, "Yes ma'am, I'm alright." She said, "I love you," and I said "I love you, too. They will be bringing me back to Georgia, so I'll see you then. Good night madear." She said, "Good night, baby." I sat there until the officer came and got me and took me to a pod that was all glass. I was upstairs. When they put me in that room, I looked out the window and saw a train track and I heard a train far off. I broke down and cried. See, I grew up by a train track and that just tore me up to hear that train. I started thinking about home and my kids. I was wondering what was going to happen to them and how they were feeling and thinking about all that had happened to me. Especially what was going to happen next. I just laid down and went to sleep. One good thing, I wouldn't be having a roommate. They were single rooms.

The officer called me out to ask me if I would like to take a shower. I stepped out and asked her where the showers were. She pointed up and I saw where the shower was. I told her, "No thank you." See, the officer's station sits up high. They look down at you, even in the shower and everybody in the pod can see you, too. I only came out to eat and I took my little birdie baths in my room. They talked about me but I didn't care.

Chapter 7

The next day they called me out. I had a visitor and for some reason, I just knew it was my brother Calvin. But it wasn't. It was Michael on the other side of the wall. He was crying! I couldn't believe it. It made me cry, too. He said, "When I came back, you were gone. Then the people told me they took you in a police car. I went to Linkie's house and she was the one who told them about you. She said she got scared. Your brother ain't shit. He talking about he didn't know you was in that much trouble. Has he come to see you?"

I told him, "I thought you were him." He put his hand up to the glass and I put mine up there. He told me, "I love you, Dianne and we will see other again." I told him, "Mike, please forget about me." He said, "It's not that easy to forget about you." He left me some money and told me goodbye. He was crying. He blew me a kiss and left. I lay on my bed feeling empty and alone. I went out when dinner came and sat there a while looking and taking in my surroundings.

Lord, where did these people come from? The whole place was glass. You could see into the next pod, which were all pregnant women. I sat and watched TV for a while and then went back up to my room. Two days later, they took me to court. The judge told me if I live in California, I could sign myself out. But since I didn't, he had to wait and see what Georgia wanted them to do.

About three weeks later they took me back in front of the judge. He told me, "Ms. Cooper, Georgia has 10 days to come get you. If they do not come for you within those 10 days, we will turn you loose. The problem with that is you cannot go back to Georgia. Do you understand?" I said, "Yes sir." Then he told me, "You may go." So I was taken back and sent to my room. After that, I was counting days. I just knew on the ninth day Georgia wasn't coming and was I ever wrong! The next morning they said, "Cooper come on, you're leaving." I got up and said, "Shit."

The officer took me down and this white guy, a blonde with a ponytail said, "Miss Cooper, I'm here to take you back to Georgia. If you try to run between here and Georgia, I will shoot you." I looked at him and I said, "If you shoot at me and miss, I will shoot you back!" He just looked at me and shook his head. He got my purse from the man behind the desk and signed some papers. He told me to turn around and he handcuffed me and we went out the door to the parking lot. I knew this was going to be a long trip. He opened the car door for me and strapped me in.

When he got to the driver's side, I noticed he was a nice looking man. He had a holster on with a nine millimeter in it. He said, "You're not what I expected." I said, "What did you expect?" He said, "Not you. What did you do?" I said, "I didn't do anything. I sure didn't do anything for Georgia to send a Governor's Warrant and a bounty hunter with a nine at me." He laughed. He said, "No seriously what did you do?"

"Man I told you, I didn't do anything." He said, "Well you don't want to tell me, fine." I sat there and looked out the window. We didn't say anything more. We arrived at Delta Airlines and he came around and helped me out the car. We walked up to the airport ticket counter. He said, "Stand right behind me and don't move." I said, "Where would I go with these cuffs on?" He gets two first class tickets to Salt Lake City. He tells me to walk in front of him. So we walk out to the plane. The pilot tells Mister Bounty Hunter that he has to take the cuffs off me before I get on the plane. The bounty hunter said, "Look, she's my prisoner and I have to get her back to Georgia. I can't take the cuffs off."

He finally gave in and told me to turn around and said, "You better not try anything." I said, "You've been looking at too much TV." He said, "No I haven't. It happened to me before." The pilot told us to get on first. He said, "When the plane lands, you two get off last."

When we got on the plane and was in the air, the stewardess asked me if I wanted anything to drink. I said "Yes, I'll have a gin on the rocks." Mister Bounty Hunter said, "No she will have a coke." I looked at him and said, "She was not taking to you." He said, "I

Dark Justice

know, but you are not having any alcoholic drinks on the plane." I told the stewardess to give me a coke and some peanuts. She smiled at me and said, "Sure thing." Then she asked him if he wanted anything. He asked for the same. We didn't talk anymore.

Soon we landed and everybody got off the plane. He put the cuffs back on me. We were at Salt Lake City Airport. We went in and went straight to the ticket counter. He bought two tickets to Atlanta, Georgia. They told him he had an hour before boarding. So he flashed his little identification and asked her where he could put me for an hour or so? She informed him they have a little room with a concrete bed in it. He put me in there and locked the door.

I just sat there thinking this shit has got to be a dream. I'm sure I will wake up soon. I was so tired while I was sitting there thinking to myself, then he opened the door. He asked me if I wanted a cigarette. I told him "Sure, thank you." He said, "Come on out." I was still handcuffed. He released one hand and left the other cuff on my other hand. He said, "Can I ask you something?" I said, "What?" and blew out my smoke. "What did you really do? You did something because they want you pretty bad.

I said "For the tenth time, I haven't done anything." He looked at me and said, "Hurry up with your smoke, we got to go." So I finished my cigarette and put my hand out so he could cuff my wrist. We went back into the airport and we had about fifteen minutes before boarding. I told him, "I need to go to the bathroom." He stood just stood there. I said, "I need my hands sir, do you mind?" A lady was coming out. He asked her if anybody else was in there. She said no. He went in with me and checked the bathroom and stood outside the stall. I said, "I still need my hand." He said, "Shit" and unlocked the one wrist.

I went in and used it and came out. Washed my hands and he cuffed me back again. We came out and went to the boarding area. He took the cuffs off again and we got on the plane. After we were seated he said, "You want to play some cards?" I said, "Why would I want to play cards? No, I don't want to play cards with you." He just turned and looked out the window.

We went up in the air and I sat and watched the movie "Beethoven" about this big dog running all over the house. After a while, we were landing in Atlanta. We got off the plane and I got handcuffed again. He went and got two tickets to Savannah, Georgia. We had about a twenty minute wait. He handcuffed me to the seat. I was sitting there with my head down. Hoping I didn't see anyone I knew and who knew me. I was so happy when he came and un-cuffed me from that seat and said, "Let's go." We got on the plane and he didn't talk at all, which was a blessing to me.

When we landed in Savannah, Georgia, two cops was there waiting on us. He turned me over to them. He took his cuffs off and they put theirs on me. He said, "Take care Coop." I said, "Yeah, right," and he was gone. The two cops put me in the back of the police car and drove me to Jesup, Georgia. When we arrived there, waiting for me was that same detective I couldn't stand. That little piece of nothing, Detective John Taylor! A Savannah, Georgia cop took off the hand cuffs and told Detective Taylor, "She's all yours." He was so happy talking about, "Well Miss Cooper, we've been looking for you. Have a seat!" I sat down at the little broken down table in this Andy Griffith jail. I was looking for Barney Fife to come out at anytime. Taylor said, "You must be very tired. You want a cup of coffee and a cigarette?" I said, "Cigarette."

He gave me a cigarette and lit it for me and said, "First, will you sign this for me? It's not anything that will hurt you. We just need you to sign this for us okay?" I signed the paper and he said, "Lock her ass up," and left out the door. The little country cop came and said, "Let's go, ma'am." He put me in a cell. I tell you it was just like the one in Mayberry. The bed, phone, shower and toilet were in the cell. It had a little black and white TV outside the cell with a broken wire hanger for an antenna.

If I hadn't been dragged half way across the world, I would have been laughing. It was about three women in the cell lying on mattresses. They brought me one and I found myself a spot. When I laid down, I went into a comatose sleep. I woke up to women playing cards and a loud TV. I got up and went behind the shower curtain where the toilet was and used the bathroom. About ten minutes later came breakfast. They also brought me a blue jumper to put on. But they let me keep my shoes. The food was good because it came from a café. After breakfast, I got up and called my mama. She was so happy to hear from me. She told me Shon was home and had been home about two months. She also told me my daughter, Juanita, was getting married.

I was so happy for my baby. Of course if I wasn't in jail, I would have found a whole lot of reasons why she should wait. Then I was told she was pregnant, which to me, didn't matter. She did better than I did. At least she graduated from high school before she got pregnant. I was so proud of my baby. I still am! "Well" I said, "Where is she? I want to talk to her." She wasn't there so I talked to my baby, Alexis. She said, "Mama where you at?" I told her "I am in jail and in a lot of trouble, but madear is going to bring you to see me." She said, "Okay mama." Then she said, "Mama, can I spend the night with you?" I told her, "No baby you can't. This is not a place for little girls." She didn't say anything for a minute. Then she said, "When is madear bringing me to see you?" I told her, "Tomorrow, okay?" She said, "Okay." I told her to let me talk to madear.

My mama said, "Baby, are you okay?" I said, "Yeah, I'm fine." She said "Where are you? I hear people and a TV." I told her I was in Jesup. She said "What?" I told her, "Yeah, they brought me here last night around 3:00 a.m. this morning." She said, "Baby, can I come and see you?" I told her "Oh yes ma'am. I told Alexis that you would bring her tomorrow." She said, "Alright baby, I'll see you tomorrow."

So I hung up and called my sister, Linda. When she answered, I said, "Linda, what's up?" She hollered, "Bitch what the hell going on?" I told her, "Hi Linda. It's nice to hear your voice too! As to what is going on, I'm in Jesup, Georgia, in a damn Barney Fife jail. So how is everybody? I heard my daughter is getting married." She said, "She is marrying Raymond. He's in the Army and you know she's pregnant." I told her, "Yes I heard. How is she?" She said, "Girl, graduation was a trip. The police were everywhere. They just knew you were going to show up. And check this, Nita was in Wal-Mart and somebody tipped the police off that you were in the shopping center. Girl, they came and arrested Juanita. They thought she was you! Madear had to go get her out and your crazy daughter thought that was funny."

I had to laugh. I could just picture that. Then she said, "How long you been in Jesup?" I told her, "I just got here last night. Linda, I have been through hell and back. This guy they had sent to get me was a damn bounty hunter. They sent a damn bounty hunter after my ass. Can you believe it? Me! Little old me." Linda said, "Girl, I know you lying! Stop lying." I said, "Girl, I am not playing. Listen, this is some funny shit. We were coming out of Atlanta airport right? I had on my funky jeans and this guy said, 'Damn! Baby got back.' The bounty hunter ran right into the glass door and was pulling his gun out his holster at the same time. I laughed at him. He said, 'What is he talking about? What does that mean?' I told him, Man, that's a song and he's talking about my ass. Lord, but that shit was funny!"

Linda said, "Girl what did he look like? Were you scared?" I said, "No, I was madder than anything. As to what the man looked like, he was tall, blonde, blue eyes and a ponytail. He also had a shoulder strap with a nine millimeter in it." Linda said, "Damn! Dianne, I'm sorry. Look, I'm coming to see you tomorrow. What can I bring you? Money? Cigarettes, matches and a perm? Can I bring you all that?" I told her "Yeah." She said, "Alright then. I'll see you tomorrow." We hung up.

When I turned around, all the girls was looking at me. I said, "Damn, may I help you?" The black girl said, "Well shit, we couldn't help but hear your conversation. That's some interesting shit." I said, "Yeah, but it's my business. But you're right." She said, "What's your name?" I said, "Dianne Cooper." She said, "My name is Janie. This is Susan and Carolyn." I said, "Hi." Carolyn said, "Is it true they brought you from California last night?" I said, "Yes it is." She said, "You're the talk of the jail." I said, "I guess I am." Susan said, "It's almost time for rec. Are you going?" I said, "Yeah, it'll be nice to be able to get out in the sun. It's been a minute for me."

Then this officer came in and stood in front of our cell. He looked at me and said, "Well look'a here. You've been playing with the big boys. You were in the newspaper and on TV. Ya'll going to rec?" They said, "Yeah." So we all came out the cell and went past the desk and out the side door. It looked like somebody's back yard. They had a tee & tee, a fence on one side for the men, and the other was for the women. The women talked to the men threw the fence. I was talking to Susan, laughing about the fence when I heard this guy say, "Hey, ain't that Dianne Cooper?" I said, "Who are you and how do you know me?" While he was coming up to the fence, I looked at him, and then I remembered him. I said, "Cash Money, what are you doing in here?" He laughed and said, "I figured you would remember me. You Diamond's woman. I read about you. Damn, how did you get caught up in this mess, man?"

"I don't know. Where do we go for visits?"

"Out here".

I said, "Out here? Suppose it rains?"

He said, "We'll cancel the visit. Do you have a bond yet?"

And I said, "No. I just came here last night."

He said, "I know. What's up with Diamond? Do y'all still talk or what?"

I said, "We alright at the moment, but for the record, I am not Diamond's woman and I haven't been in a while. We are just good friends and we look out for each other." Then the officer said Rec was over. He said to me, "I'll be talking to you."

The next day was a visiting day. I was coming out when, who do I see while passing the desk? My brother Donnell, talking trash to the cop. Telling him, "I am an officer like you and if I see one scratch on my sister, you're gonna answer to me." I said, "Donnell, please don't make it hard for me," and went back out the door. When we walked around the back, they would put our money in an envelope with our name on it and they would bring it to us later. I looked and I couldn't believe my eyes. They had put up a yellow rope tied across the front of the fence so I couldn't get close to it. Then they had the Forest Rangers, the fire department and their little police outside the gate with rifles and guns.

I asked Janie if all that was for me. She said, "Yeah, girl. You the biggest thing that ever hit this little country jail." I felt so bad. Then I saw my family hit the corner. I couldn't hug them or anything. They just had to stand outside that fence and talk to me. My mama was smiling as she was just happy to lay eyes on me. My daughters looked lost and hurt. My sisters, just like my mama, was just as happy to see me in one piece. They told me that they gave the cops a big bag of stuff for me. They even brought me some soda, chips, and a whole bunch of junk! They told me all about what was going on and what people were saying about me. I didn't care about that. I wanted to go home to my girls.

My girls asked me, "Mama when is they going to let you come home?" I told them the truth. "Babies I have no idea." And I didn't. My family tried to be strong, but I knew they were sick about all this. My son showed up with his boys: Lenzy, Hester, and Gator, my little first cousin. When I saw them, I let them have it. I told them, "Man, don't ya'll come back up in here dressed like a drug dealer. Look at you, all that damn jewelry on. Don't do that no more." He said,

"Okay ma." Then he said, "Ma you coming out of this, don't worry. Everybody knows you ain't have nothing to with drugs. You don't even know how to sell drugs."

I said, "I know, Shon. Keep an eye on your sisters."

"They gone be alright and don't worry. Juanita's wedding going to be just like as if you were there." I said, "Thank you, baby." Then I asked, "So is your dad going to do his part?" Shon said, "I'm going to take him to buy his tux." I said, "So you got to buy his tux?" He said, "Yeah ma, I don't mind."

So I stood there and talked to the family and when my visit was over, we all went back to our little Andy Griffith cell. We played cards until dinner. Then they brought us our money bags. My family truly did me justice back then. I didn't want for anything back then. I was in that jail for five months. The day of my daughter's wedding, I ran that thing from the jail. Shon wasn't there because the police had him off the streets against the wall, so I called her uncle Davis and asked where Joseph, his brother was. Nobody could find him. So I asked Davis if he would give Juanita away for me, and he said, "It's not a problem."

Then I called the house to talk to Nita and she was upset. "Ma, I can't find daddy or Shon. I'll just have to walk myself down the aisle." I told her, "No baby, I got you. Your uncle Davis is going to give you away. You need to be getting ready to go to the church, okay? I'll call you after the wedding and I love you." She said, "Thank you ma and I love you too." I told her to put her aunt Gloria on the phone. Gloria said, "Hey girl, your daughter is about to be a married woman." I asked her where Alexis was. She said, "She's in there with madear." I said, "Get her dressed and have her sit on the sofa until it's time to go. You all are cutting it close." She said, "Oh yeah, you're right. Okay I am going to hang up. Call back later." I told her, "You can count on it." So I hung up, and went to play cards until I thought the wedding was over.

The card games kept my mind off the fact that I was missing my daughter's wedding. When I called back, my sister, Maureen answered. She said, "Your daughter made a beautiful bride. She cried because you weren't there. Shon didn't make the wedding. The police finally let him go. He's gone looking for his dad. I'm going to head out to the reception." I said, "Tell Nita I am proud of her, okay?" She said, "I'll do that and you take care, baby sis." I said, "You too." Then I lit me a cigarette and went back to the card game. I didn't call home for a couple of days. When I did, my mama told me they were coming to visit and she was bringing Alexis. So I was outside writing when I spotted this little girl walking fast. It was Alexis. I stood there with a big smile on my face. They still had the Forest Rangers and the yellow rope, which I wasn't suppose to go across. My baby stood on the other side of that fence smiling at me. She said, "Hey mama!" I said, "Hey baby, give mama some sugar." She looked at all those men standing there watching me. I got so mad. That's when I walked under the rope and told her again, "Give mama a kiss."

When she did, one of the men grabbed her to pull her back from the fence and she started hollering "Mama!" I lost it. I went to cursing and trying to go over the fence. My sister, Linda and my mama had hit the corner by then. I was yelling, "Get your motherfucking hands off my baby! I'll kill you! Take your damn hands off her." The men on the other side started cursing. Some cops came and snatched me off the fence and threw me on the ground. I screamed, "Linda get Alexis out of here and don't bring her back." She was crying. Linda covered her eyes so she didn't see them taking me back in. Some had my feet, while the others had my shoulders. I was kicking and screaming. The men were yelling, "Leave her alone!" and "Don't do that in front of her kid. Leave the woman alone! Turn her loose."

Then they took me in hand cuffs and put me a room that looked like a bank vault. Now I was kind of scared because I was by myself and they could do anything to me back there. Who was going to tell? I was crying and looking around this vault. I had a bed and a toilet. I sat there for about ten minutes when I heard somebody say "Miss Cooper?"

"Yeah," I said.

"You alright?"

"Yeah."

He said, "Look one of us is going to check on you every fifteen minutes, okay? We ain't gonna let them do nothing to you, alright?" I said, "Thank you." Then Cash Money said, "Don't worry Dianne, we got you." I said, "Thank you all."

I sat there on that bed crying and thinking about what just happened. All I wanted was a kiss from my baby. Lord, I miss my kids. Why is this happening to me? Why are you letting this happen? I ain't did nothing! And then I would start crying again. They left me in there for a couple days. When they brought me out, the officer said, "You almost started a riot in here, getting those men all upset." I told him I didn't do anything.

When they took me back to the cell, everybody was gone. I was the only female in the cell. One night, I looked over to the other cell. It was an old white haired lady in there. She was sitting in the chair, just looking at me. I waved at her and she waved back. A run-around came to the door and handed me a letter and said, "That lady sent this." I read the note and it said, "Miss Cooper, it's gonna be okay. Don't worry about your journey, it's gonna be okay. You are not alone." I looked over at her and said, "How do you know me? Who are you?" She didn't say anything.

At mail time I got a letter from Michael. I was so surprised. He also had sent me a picture. He told me he had Dianne fever and he had called my family and talked to them. He also told me in the letter that he had seen my brother Calvin and he was feeling really bad about all the trouble I was in and he didn't know about this. Said he was sorry that he didn't take care of me and look out for me better.

Michael was mad at my brother, but I wasn't. I know my brother and he didn't understand. I know he loves me. It was okay but he couldn't stop it. They still would have gotten me.

After I was finished reading Mike's letter, I looked up and saw they had brought me some company, a black girl named Shirley. She came and I said, "Hi, what's your name?" She told me, and then I said, "I'm Dianne." She said, "Nice to meet you, Dianne." She took the other bed. She told me about what they had arrested her for. She was caught boosting (stealing). She did that to pay for her drug habit. I forgot all about the old lady until the next day, which was Sunday. I had my breakfast and then she crossed my mind. I looked over there and she was gone. I asked the run-around what happened to that old lady. He said, "What old lady?" I said, "The old lady that wrote me this note you gave me." He said, "Stop playing. Ain't nobody been in that cell and I didn't bring you no note."

Chapter 8

Well, about that lady. I never saw her again and it seemed nobody saw her but me. The run-around said, "I promise you Dianne, I didn't bring you anything." That still bothers me up to this day. I told my mama about it on the phone and she told me that was God's way of letting me know that He's with me. My attitude was yeah, whatever. I didn't tell her that. I kept that to myself and said, "Yeah, I see. Thank you, madear."

That night the officer told me that I was going to have a bond hearing. I called my mama back. She told me not to worry, she had me a lawyer and he was on his job. She told me to call her back in about thirty minutes because she wanted to check and see what time the hearing was. So while I was waiting to call her back, I was talking to Shirley. Telling her about my kids and Michael. About the time I figured my mama was through talking to Mr. Mitchell, the lawyer, I called. She answered and said, "Baby, he said the hearing is at 1:30 p.m." I said, "Alright Madear." Then I said, "Madear are you okay?" She said, "Yeah baby I been praying real hard for you." I said, "Thank you madear, I know you have. I have to go so I'll see you tomorrow."

She said, "Sleep with angels, baby." I said, "You too, good night."

The next morning I woke up early. I was happy. I thought I was going home. When we got there, they had already had the hearing. The hearing was at 12:30 p.m. My lawyer had lied to my mama. I met her outside. She was waiting just to get a glimpse of me. I said, "Madear, what's wrong?" The cop was with me. She said, "Baby they done had the hearing. They want a hundred and fifty thousand dollars." I said "Why mama? Why did he lie to you? Did you pay the lawyer?" She said, "I gave him a thousand dollars." I said, "Madear, get your money back. I'll get me a public defender, don't worry."

So they took me back to jail. They made sure I didn't get bonded out. They told my mama it would be at 1:30 and they had it at 12:30 without me or my family present. I made it back before rec. I saw Cash Money during rec and he said, "That was so damn dirty. I should be getting out tomorrow. When I get out, I promise you, I'll bond you out if you promise to marry me." I laughed because I didn't think he was serious, so I said, "If you get me out, it's a deal."

That next evening, the run-around came and said "Dianne, Cash Money came to bail you out, but they didn't let him because the U.S. Marshall is out at the desk to pick you up." All I could say was, "Shit!" He wasn't gone a minute when they pulled me out and took me up front. Sure enough, there stood the feds with paper in their hands. They said, "Miss Cooper, we are here for you to sign these papers. You have been indicted."

I remember my mama trying to explain "indicted" to me on the phone when I was in Sacramento. I just looked up at them and signed the papers. After I signed them, they took me back to my cell. The run-around had half of it right. Cash did try to bail me out, and they didn't let him because they came to indict me. So all the shit I had been through and I wasn't even indicted yet. Is that legal? This is what I was thinking.

Shirley was sitting, reading a book. She had a couple more on her bunk. I went to go to the phone when Shirley told she was going home the next day. I looked down at her feet. She had on some dirty Keds, so I told Shirley to change shoes with me. I had a pair of suede ankle boots. She smiled and said "Are you serious?" I told her, "Yeah. Hell, they ain't gonna do me no good where I'm going. Here girl." She said, "Thank you Dianne. This is the nicest thing anyone has ever done for me. I will never forget you." I said, "Sure you will, as soon as you get your next high. Here. Take the damn shoes."

So we switched shoes and then I went to call my mama. When I called, Linda answered the phone. I said, "Hi girl, what's up?" She said, "The police came in about 5:00 a.m. and took Shon. They also locked up Mattie, Willie, Doll, James, Notfire, Lester, Lenzy, and Humpy. Girl they got everybody last night." I said, "Oh my God! Where is madear?"

"Dianne, madear is in the hospital in ICU. She had a massive heart attack. They ain't expecting her to make it. I'm sorry baby sis.

When they locked you up, I thought she was going to have one. Then they came and got Shon. Well that was too much for her."

"Oh God," I said, "Lord please." Linda was crying and I started crying. I told her, "I'll talk to you later." I got up on my bed and I cried so hard that the police came in and said they had called for someone to give me a shot. I didn't answer and I didn't stop crying. I cried all that night. I cried myself to sleep. The next morning, I couldn't half see because my eyes were so swollen. I didn't want to eat. I started crying again. I felt so bad and hurt around my heart. I felt like I had let my mama and my girls down. "Lord, I am so sorry. Please don't take my mama from me. Lord, please don't take my mama, she's all I got." That's all I kept saying.

I managed to get myself together to get up and use the phone. Maureen answered. I said, "Maureen how is madear?"

"She's better. They are moving her into a room. They are taking her out of ICU." I can't tell you how good I felt. All I could do was start crying again and say, "Thank you Jesus." Maureen said, "The old lady is a fighter, Dianne. Girl I was so scared she was gone, but she's going to make it." I said, "Yeah, I'll talk to you later, sis. I love you." She said, "I love you too, baby sis." I stood there a minute, just looking at the phone, then Shirley said, "Dianne, everything alright?" I said, "Yeah, everything's fine. My mama is gonna be okay." Then the officer came in and told Shirley to pack up because she was leaving. I told her to take care of herself. She said, "I will." We hugged and she got her stuff and left.

I went and sat on the chair and cut our little TV on. I sat and watched it for a very long time. I couldn't tell you what was on. I was just watching it. Soon the cart with junk food came around. I bought me some cookies. I had a soda in my goodie bag. I got back on my bunk and started reading this gangster book. Mail came. I received another letter from Michael. I laughed. I told him to go on with his life. He's determined to hang on, but I know in the end he will stop writing. For now, I'll just enjoy it while I can. I did have a lot of fun with him. He taught me how to catch the buses and we would go to the park a lot. He loved to dance. I must say, I do miss him. Then I started thinking about my girls. Lord, what must they be thinking? I hope they don't hate me. I couldn't deal with that. I love them so much. Dinner came. I ate, took a shower and got back on my bed and went to sleep.

I was awakened by the officer. He said, "Cooper pack up. You're leaving. The Marshalls are here for you." I said, "Alright." He said, "You got five minutes. I'll send your clothes to you." I got up, brushed my teeth and washed my face. I didn't worry about taking a shower. I knew wherever I was going the first thing they would do is strip me of my clothes and give me a shower. He stood next to the bar with a bag and said, "Here Cooper, now hurry up. We don't want to keep the big boys waiting." I didn't even answer him. I just took the bag and went behind the shower curtain and put my clothes on. It felt good to put my jeans on. When I came back from behind the curtain, he wasn't there. I put the blue jumper on and waited on the man.

He told me I couldn't take any goodies with me. I couldn't even take my cigarettes! Now I was upset about that. I was glad I only had half a pack. I said, "Man, where am I going now?" He said, "I can't tell you that." I said, "Why?" He said, "We don't suppose to tell you." He unlocked the door and I went out. There were two U.S. Marshalls that stood at the front; one female and one male. The man said, "Miss Cooper, You are a popular lady. Turn around please." The female cop put the hand cuffs on then he shackled my feet. I looked at them and said, "Do you have to put them on me?" She said, "Yes we do. We want to make sure you don't run. I hear you got a little rabbit in you." She had a nasty smile. You knew then not to say anything more. This lady was not very nice at all.

We left out. I had a hard time trying to walk in those shackles and the hand cuffs were so damn tight. I wanted to ask them to loosen them a little but that lady, each time she looked back at me she had a look like I killed her mama or something. So I kept quiet and just looked out the window and said to myself, "Well girl, you might as well stop feeling sorry for yourself because nobody cares and if they did, they can't help you. And it looks like God ain't got His mind on you at the moment. You are on your own. Stop crying too, you are not a child." At that moment, I made up in my mind, I would never cry again about nothing and if I did, nobody would know. As far as I was concerned, it was all about trying to save my child. Nothing and nobody else mattered. If you didn't birth me and I didn't birth you, then fuck you and fuck the world. I kept that mentality for about two and a half years.

I was looking out the window letting my mind race when I saw the sign Brunswick, Georgia. I wonder why are they bringing me here? We rode a little ways and then I saw the Brunswick Detention Center. He pulled around to the back and unlocked the car door. He opened it and the lady said, "Alright Miss Cooper, let's go." I said, "I need some help." She said, "Oh you can do it. Swing your foot out and pull yourself up." I looked at her with so much hate and in my mind I was saying bitch if you knew what I wanted to do to your monkey ass! I just focused on getting out of that back seat. I did like she said and got up. We went to the back door.

When I walked in, the first person I saw, handcuffed to a chair was my cousin, Hattie. When she looked up and saw me the expression on her face was priceless. You could have bought her for a dime. The fear of me just made my day. I went toward her. She went to rocking, trying to get up. I said, "You big bitch. I am going to beat the hell out of you!" I couldn't run because of the shackles on my feet and I couldn't swing on her because of the hand cuffs, but I went to wobbling toward her with murder on my mind. The feds pulled me back and called another officer and told him to get Miss Hattie before she has a heart attack in that chair. They came and got her and locked me up in the bullpen. Before they did that, they took the shackles and handcuffs off. I was happy about that, but I was still highly pissed at Hattie. How could she do that? Not that we were ever that close. She was very close with my sister, Maureen. But man, we were still family. How could she use me like that?

They kept me in the bullpen, a room that looks like a big cage. It had a toilet and a bench to sit on. For over an hour I was watching people come in and out. They had some men locked up in a bullpen on the other side across from me. After another thirty minutes, they came and got me. First they asked for my mother and father's name, my address, how many brothers and sisters I had, how many living, ages, my kids and their ages, how many, my weight, how tall, any marks on my body. Man, they were personal. Then the finger printing, now they had a hard time doing that because I couldn't just let them do it. I kept trying to help when he would say, "Don't move your thumb. Just stay still and let me do it." For some reason, I wouldn't. Well we finally got that done, and then they put me in the shower. They took my clothes, put me in a red jumper and took me to the pod. The first person I saw was Mattie Jones. She looked up and smiled when she saw me. She said, "Girl we been waiting on you. Diamond said don't worry about nothing, you going to be alright." When she said that, I got all happy.

See, I trusted Diamond. If he said it, then it was so. I said, "Okay, where is Niecy Doll?" She pointed over her shoulder and said, "Up there." The officer had given me my room. My room was next to Niecy Doll's room. I asked Mattie, "Have you seen Shon?" She said. "Yeah, he was waiting on you too." I went and buzzed the officer and asked her how I can get in touch with my son. She told me she was bringing me a paper to fill out and then I could see him on Tuesdays and Thursdays.

Let me back up to the point before they took me to the pod. It was four other girls and I who were being processed in after we had dressed out. The man standing by the elevator said, "As you walk by, give me your number." The girls were giving the man their number and when he got to me he said, "Last name?" I said, "Cooper." Then he said, "Number?" I said "What number are you talking about?" He said "Your number." I had no understanding so I gave the only number I knew, which is my social security number. He said, "What kind of number is that?" I said, "That's my social security number." He said, "Dianne girl, this is your number, 08087-021. Remember it because that as of now has become your name." I said, "My name? So I am not a person?" He said, "Not anymore, you're a number!"

I didn't think much about what that officer said because to me I was and will always be a person. He was out of his rabbit ass mind as far as I was concerned. I followed the girls and the officer up to the pod. That's where I saw Mattie sitting there. Like I said, my room was next to Niecy Doll's. Mattie didn't like Niecy Doll and Niecy Doll didn't like Mattie. And Diamond couldn't stand Mattie, but he had to deal with her because of Luscious, known as Humpy who by the way, was Mattie's husband. Humpy took Diamond under his wings and taught him the ropes. Diamond had great respect for Humpy. When I met him, I understood why. Humpy was a very nice person. He was a lot older than Mattie. To him, Diamond was more like a prodigy.

I saw right off that between Niecy Doll and Mattie it was going to be some problems. I went up to my room and looked out the window. It was a park right across the street and I had a good view. I would stand there for hours sometimes and daydream. I left the window and went to the phone. When I got through, crazy Niecy Doll was standing there, smiling. Talking about "Dianne girl, we knew you was coming. I know Diamond is glad you're here." I said, "Girl what happened? Why are all of you here?" She said, "Your cousin Hattie is in the pod on the other side. She is the only one with a tape recorder. She done told those people everything. She's the reason we're all here."

Mattie came over and stood by me and said, "A couple of nights ago they came and got all of us. We were in the Ware County jail, then they brought us here. They're looking for Leroy." Niecy Doll said, "Yeah it's a lot of them that should be here, but ain't. Like Kimmy Nite and your cousin, Jenny. Why they ain't locked up in here?" I said, "Man, we gonna be alright as soon as we go to court. They will see that this is crazy." Mattie said, "None of this would have happened if Duck hadn't killed that woman."

Mattie was angry, so I said, "Mattie what kind of form I got to fill out to get a visit with Shon?" She said, "When the officer comes in to bring our dinner, I'll get one." I said, "Man, this is a hell of a place to spend Thanksgiving. It's bad enough I had to turn thirty five in that damn Mayberry jail." One of the women called over to Mattie. Mattie said, "Gail come here, I want to introduce you to somebody." Gail came over and Mattie said, "This is Dianne, Diamonds girlfriend." I said, "Hi Gail, my name is Dianne Cooper." She said, "Mattie said you two been knowing each other a long time." I said, "We been knowing each other. I used to work at the same nursing home with Mattie, and also when I married Joseph, my husband, his parents lived next door to Mattie." I didn't say I used to buy weed from Mattie when she lived next door in a trailer. Ha! She said, "Oh," and then Niecy Doll went over to talk to some other girls.

When she walked off Mattie said, "Dianne, look at them women Niecy Doll talking to. Don't go over there. You know we don't hang around women like that." I said, "Mattie what are you talking about, I'm not like that. People are people. You don't hang around with people like that, but I do. Who is she supposed to be hanging with?" Mattie said, "She's not like them." For some reason Mattie always tried to be more than she was. She really didn't deal too much with me until I started dating her husband's partner. Before then, I was one of those people she didn't deal with. She was really my sister's friend, not mine. Man, Mattie was so snobbish. I couldn't deal with her sometimes.

Mattie told me I could write Shon a letter, and when mail call comes I could give it to the officer. So I got an envelope and paper from her and wrote Shon and Diamond. Then I got a store visit and filled it out. I still had money from Jesup so I was able to get me some things. I also got me a radio. I got to know a few ladies there, and there was one who had HIV. She had twin girls. Most of everybody stayed away from her. I liked her. I spent most of my time with Niecy Doll. It was one girl in there named Sandra and she would always be with Niecy Doll. When I came around she would leave. I could never understand why. Then one day Niecy Doll said, "Dianne, Sandra is one of Diamond's women." I said, "Really?" She said, "Yeah. She was talking about him and all the things they used to do." I said "Then all she talked about was the cocaine and weed and the $81 he gave her after she went down on him." Niecy Doll laughed. She said, "How you know?" I said, "I know Diamond."

So I went and talked to the girl to let her know she wasn't the first and wouldn't be the last. But the only woman that Diamond cared about was me. Only because he knows that I will always be there for him, and I knew if I truly needed him he would be there for me, too. I knew this, so it didn't bother me. Sandra and I got to be alright with each other. When she left, she put fifteen dollars on my books. I took the receipt and put it in an envelope, and sent it around there with a note. It said, "Hey baby look at this. One of your women left me some money on my books." Niecy Doll was hollering when I did that. She said, "Girl you're crazy as hell. Diamond is going to be pissed off." I said, "If he was in front of me right now, he might get pissed on."

The officer told me, "Cooper, you got a visit." I couldn't wait! I hurried out. I was disappointed when I saw the glass and behind it was my son. My heart broke into a thousand pieces. I haven't seen him in a while. He had turned twenty and I had turned thirty five. I went in and picked up the phone. The first thing that he said was, "Ma, I am so happy to you. You done picked up some weight." I said, "Yeah it was that country cooking I was getting in Jesup." We would have fried chicken, dressing, greens and cornbread every Sunday, and a big old cup of lemon tea. I ate good. He said, "It looks good on you. You don't need to gain anymore. Diamond's going to like that weight on you. Look, the boys told me to tell you we all want you out of this because you for real the only one that doesn't fit. Ma, you ain't never been in jail or nothing. You shouldn't be here, and it's all because Hattie tricked Diamond into sending you instead of Duck. Ma, I kept telling Diamond Duck was going to be his downfall. Duck act like Diamond was his daddy. He didn't want anybody around him. He couldn't stand me and Diamond's relationship. Man I messed up when I introduced that nigger. I hate I did that, Ma. Listen, just tell them people Diamond told you to pick up a package from Hattie and don't say anything else. You gone get out of this."

I said. "What about you?" We gone get you out of this. I can't let you go to jail. You too young to go to prison. I got to get you out of this." He said, "Ma, you tripping. We gone be alright. Listen we get to talk every Tuesday and Thursday and if you go to church, I get to see you."

"Shon be careful," I said. "Please don't get in any trouble. We got to get out of here. Alright?" He said, "Okay Ma." Then he said, "Kawanda is pregnant, and Tasha said her lil girl is also mine." I said, "Shon, how in the hell? When did all this happen? You got three kids?" He said, "Two and one on the way." Boy! He said, "Kawanda and Nita both got pregnant at the same time." I said, "I guess I'll call Kawanda when I get back round there. Tell the boys I said hello and not to worry about me. I'm okay. I'm in here with Niecy Doll and Mattie. They keep Hattie on the other side." Shon said, "They know to keep Hattie away from you. Ma, have you seen your Lawyer yet?" I told him, "No I haven't, have you?" He said "Yeah. I wonder why they haven't got you one, everybody else have already seen their lawyer. Ma, you need to check into that." I told him "Okay baby, I will. Love ya!" He said, "Love you more," and hung up the phone. The officer took him out. My heart broke again into a thousand pieces.

The officer took me back to the pod, and Mattie asked how my visit went. I told her just fine. I told her what Shon said about telling them about the package. She said "Yeah that's all you need to say. You know I would never tell them people nothing to hurt Shon or you." I said, "Mattie, what are you talking about?" She said, "I would never say nothing to hurt you or Shon." I just said, "Okay. I would never say anything to hurt you either."

Then the officer came and got me again. I thought, wonder what that is about? They took me into a room and this man was sitting in there like he had an attitude. He said, "Come in, Miss Cooper." They had cuffs on me this time. I sat down. He said "I know all about you." I said, "That's good, but I don't know anything about you. First if you don't mind, who are you and what do you want from me?" He said, "Your probation officer and I are here to ask you some questions." I said, "Didn't you say you know all about me? So why do you need to ask me some questions?" He said, "I heard you were a smart ass." "Well," I replied, "I question that, because if I was smart I wouldn't be talking to you." He said, "Look, I need to get this over with. I've already talked to your son."

That's when I got quiet. Then I said, "Okay what questions?"

"First, when was the last time you worked?"

I said, "October 16, 1990."

"Why did you leave your job?"

I told him, "I didn't leave my job. I got into an accident and was on vacation for two weeks and sick leave the week after."

He looked up at me from writing. "I didn't know that."

I said, "You're kidding."

He just looked at me and said, "Do you drink?"

I said, "Yes, I drink gin and Miller Light in the bottle only."

He said, "Do you do drugs?"

I said, "I do weed, no lacing, just weed by itself."

He said "Did you ever sell drugs?"

"No"

"Have you ever worked for Eugene Edmond?"

"No, I didn't have to. Anything I wanted from him, all I had to do was ask, and the same goes for him."

"You love Eugene Edmond?"

"Yes I do"

"How could you love a man who cheated on you?"

"The same way a man can love me when I am married to someone else."

"Okay Miss Cooper, that's all that I need." Then he hit the door for the officer to come and get me.

When I went back Mattie said, "What did they want with you?" I said, "It was my probation officer. That man had a lot of attitude. He took one look at me and it was like he got mad about something. Look Mattie, I am going to fix me a cup of coffee." Mattie said, "How can you drink that stuff black like that with no sugar?" I said, "I drink coffee, it's not a problem, girl."

While I was walking up the steps, I said "Where is Niecy Doll?" She said, "I think she's in the room with one of her new friends." I asked her, "Which one?" She said, "The one down from you." I went in my room and got my cup and was in the middle of fixing my coffee when they said, "Mail." While I was waiting, I put my cup in the microwave. Sure enough I got a letter from Shon and Diamond. I went and sat down to read my mail. They both talking about taking it to court and keeping my mouth shut. Shon said that he thinks Kitchen is going to tell. He told me that he is acting like he is crazy around there, chasing roaches. This other guy, I never did see him, some Spanish guy, was around there eating soap. They had to take him to the hospital.

Damn, that's sad, but I guess when you're scared that's what you'll do. Well, I didn't do anything and I am taking mine to trial, me and my son. I'm not letting him go to jail. I saw Niecy Doll reading her mail and I went over where she was. I asked her, "Who wrote you?" She said, "Willie. He said Diamond said that he hope Humpy don't break. He said that's the only one that could take him down. He's worried about the state murder charge. He said that he believe that he can beat that one. He's worried about you. Are they going to let you have a visit?" I said, "Don't think so. That officer said husband and wife, mother and son, brother and sister and Diamond don't fit any of them. So that ain't happening."

Niecy Doll said, "Well that's what he said. Anyway listen, I want me some popcorn. You want some? I can't eat the whole bag."

"Yeah. Go and pop the popcorn. I'm going in my room. Come on in there when you're finished." I went and looked out the window. It was a wedding going on, and it was beautiful. That was the first time I have ever seen a black and white wedding. The gown was white with a black and white train, and a white veil with a black rose on top. When Niecy Doll walked in, I showed it to her and we ate popcorn and watched the wedding out the window.

The next week, Niecy Doll had a visit and this guy came. That night he came to her window and how about she had his friend come to my window. I tell you that man scared the shit out of me! They called him Red. One night I was lying on my bed, and I heard something and I got up to look out the window. It was Red. He had rode a bicycle up to the darn jail, and he was drunk. I went to the window and I said, "Red, what are you doing?" That drunk man said, "I was thinking about you, so I came to see how you were doing." I said, "Wait a minute." I went to put my slides on my feet. I told Red, "You're drunk. Go home and get out of my window."

The next morning I told Niecy Doll about Red and she laughed at me so hard. We were eating breakfast when the commissary officer came in. She said, "I need somebody to work in the commissary, but you have to be Federal. State can't work." Didn't nobody say anything. She said, "Coop what about you?" I said, "Sure, I'll do it." She said, "Put your tennis shoes on. So that day I started working and I loved it. I got the chance to be out of there. Mattie, all she did was watch soaps. And Niecy Doll, all she did was be messy. Those other girls for some reason didn't like me. Mattie's friend, all she did was complain about how she wanted to go home. So yeah, working with Dena worked for me.

During those times the fed really started messing with me. The first time was two weeks after I got there. I got a visit from my family. I even saw my cousin Clarence Kenney, as well as my friend Sandra Davis. That girl and I had some good times together. It was like so many on the other side of the glass. I hated them seeing me like that. I really hated my girls seeing me in that monkey suit, but at least I got to see them. Everybody was just looking at me more than they were talking. To be honest, I was glad when the visit was over. Reason being, I could tell that they were feeling sorry for me and themselves.

My brother Calvin came, but he didn't have an ID. The truth was, he wasn't paying child support and was scared that he would get arrested, so he stayed outside. I waved at him out the window. He looked so sad. I know that he was feeling guilty about me being in there. Which he should feel guilty anyway. After they left, I went into my little room and I was thinking about my visit when they called me out and it was the police. I walked in and the game started.

"Miss Cooper, how are you?" I said, "How do you think I am?" Then her attitude changed. "We came here to help you. If you don't want to help yourself, you will never see your little girl again." I said, "Now when did you become God?"

"Bitch, I said you need to do something with that mouth of yours! Now sit there and listen to what I have to say."

I said, "I got your bitch. Who do you think I am? Ya mama!"

He told the officer, "Get this black bitch outta here. Lets' see how bad you are when you don't ever see your daughter again."

I screamed, "Fuck you!" I was so mad that I was shaking. When I walked in, Niecy Doll and Mattie said, "Dianne are you alright?" I said, "Yeah." Then I told them what the prosecutor said to me. Niecy Doll said, "Dianne don't let them get to you." I told her, "He didn't get to me, he just pissed me off. Who does he think he is calling me that? What he's really mad about is that I'm not scared. When he came at me, I got back with him, and guess what? Every time they call me out there I'm going to do the same thing. Fuck him! Man, I am so tired of these people."

Then one of the girls who lived downstairs said, "That's what you get. You come in here thinking you're better than everybody else." I said, "Niecy Doll who is that and what is she talking about?" The girl said, "I'm talking about you."

I said, "Lady, you don't even know me. What's your problem?"

She said, "You."

By this time, she and three of her friends had come over. They stood there like they could eat me alive. I said, "Niecy Doll, "Do you know what they are talking about?" She said "No, but they are not going to fuck with you."

About two hours later they pulled me out again and this time Diamond was there. It was a man standing behind him. I said, "Damn, what's up baby? Been a long time, how are you?" He said, "I'm alright. It's been a long time, but I am going to be alright. The only one that could hurt us is Humpy, and I don't think he is going to say anything. He isn't about to let Manny go to prison if he can help it, so don't worry. You alright?"

I said, "Just stay strong, okay? What about Shon?" He said "Shon is going to be alright. We are going to handle this together, okay?" I said, "Yeah, alright. Diamond, where is Tamela and why isn't she in here?"

He said, "I told them people, but they do what they want to do. When I was getting processed, I thought that was her crying and talking her butt off. Baby I told you, these people do what they want to."

Then the man said, "Alright, let's go."

The next day I was working at the commissary. I see that one of the officers had brought Diamond up here to see me. He said, "Hi baby, I got one of the officers to bring me here so that I could get my commissary and so I could look at you." I should have known something was up because right after that they moved him out of the jail along with Hattie and Niecy Doll.

When Shon wrote me and told me that, a little fear came into me. They wanted to keep me and Diamond separated. As long as he was around me they wouldn't be able to handle him. As they moved him, all hell broke loose. They kept Diamond for about two months, Niecy Doll about a month. I had been telling Mattie that Niecy Doll was going to snitch. If she said anything about my son, so help me I am going to beat the breaks off her. I can't believe her. She talking about everybody else, and she is telling all she knows and don't know.

She was the only one to get bond. And then she turned around and got in trouble. She had cocaine on her within so many feet of a school district so they brought her back. Now they come and snatch her out along with Diamond. When Niecy Doll came back, those females had no problem telling her what I had been saying. She looked at me funny for a moment. I said, "Niecy Doll, where did they take you, girl? We have been worried about you." She said they took her to a country jail and Diamond went somewhere else. "Diamond said that he will explain it to you when he sees you."

At mail call I received a letter from him. He was explaining how the Government let you make a deal and you do not have to go to trial. I didn't get what he was talking about. I was called out again and the same man with the attitude was there, and so was another one. He said, "Ms. Cooper we need to ask you some questions, please." He had a folder full of pictures and asked me did I know any of the people? I looked through it and for real, I didn't know any of them. Then he gave me a sheet of paper with a lot of names on it and asked me did I know any of them. I read some of them and I couldn't believe it.

Back then I was a people person. I loved crowds, the club, and the whole thing. The people's names on that list was supposed to be my friends and a lot of them relatives. I told him, "Yeah, I know some of them." He said, "Show us the ones you know." So I called them out.

He said, "Did any of them work for Edmond?" I told him I didn't know if they worked for Edmond or not. The other one, Mr. Attitude said, "I told you that she wasn't going to help, that's why I got something on her ass." He got up and opened the door and my son was standing there handcuffed. He said, "Now what do you have to say, Miss Smart Ass?"

Shon said, "I'm alright. Don't say nothing. Ma, don't say nothing. We are going to be alright! We will ride this out together, trust me Ma." I looked at my baby and then looked at the man and said, "Fuck you. Kiss my dead grandmother's ass. Now take me back!" When I got back, it was time for them to lock us down. They were getting ready to bring meals. Oh, I was hot! I wanted to call home to see if Diamond or anyone had called Linda. Finally they let us out. When they popped the door, I was out and running to the phone. I called Linda and she said that Diamond had called and he was making a plea because Humpy sold him out and he doesn't have a choice. He said he made a deal for me and Shon. I said, "What?" She said, "Yeah, that's what he said."

"Linda I don't understand. He ain't made nothing for me. I got my visit with Shon tomorrow and I'll see what he wants to do." Linda said, "Dianne, you sure you know what you're doing?" I said, "I know I'm not pleading to something I didn't do. Look, the officer want me, so I have to get off the phone. I'll call you back later, alright?"

I hung up the phone and went to see what the officer wanted. She said, "Miss Cooper, you need to come with me. Your lawyer is here to see you." I said, "Well, I already have a lawyer." I'm ready. I feel better about things now. See, in my head, I had the idea that when I take this thing to court, they will see that I was used and I didn't have anything to do with this shit. I was looking for my lawyer to do some Perry Mason stuff. She sent me back to the same room and there sat this short man looking like Andy Griffith's son with the same red hair.

He told me his name. "Hello Miss Cooper, my name is Charles Johnson. I am your lawyer. Look, I have never handled a criminal case before, but I am a divorce lawyer. So just work with me. They told me they planned on taking this case to court in two weeks." I said, look I didn't do anything." He said, "First of all, look at this list of names. The ones that are marked are the ones that plan to testify against you." I said, "These are my people." I saw my cousin Johnny Bell, Kate Nite, Jackie Kenny, and I couldn't believe Hattie. Again I said, "These are my people." He said, "Tell me what you know about them."

So we went down the list. He asked me did they hang around Edmond, who worked for him and who didn't. See, I could not answer those questions because I did not know the answer. That is what the prosecution didn't understand, and they didn't believe me. The only person that believed me was my lawyer, and he didn't know what the hell he was doing. All he wanted me to do was take a plea. I told him that I was not taking no damn plea. I didn't do anything. He asked me, "Who drove you to the airport?" I wouldn't say. He said, "I am your lawyer. Who drove you?" I said, "I will tell you, but if you tell anyone I told you this I will say that you're lying. Diamond's mama drove me and his little brother was in the car."

I never told anyone, not even my son, reason being who would it help? It wouldn't have helped me. His lil brother? No! I was not about to let them break up another mother and son. That little boy needed his mother. Oh, I know that my kids need me too, but the police already had me.

He asked, "Why didn't you tell them that when they asked you?" He went through his papers and pulled out the statement from when I said some friends of Diamond's drove me to the airport. I had told them I didn't know their names. Yeah, I lied and I would do it again. "I didn't want to hurt anybody, even though it look like everybody doing their best to hurt me." My lawyer told me, "Cooper, I know you have asked for a separate trial, but they said you can't have one. You just can't. Look, you are the only one that has never been in trouble before, and the only crime that I see you committed was loving the wrong man, but this is the plea bargain that I have for you."

He hands me the papers. After I looked at them I said, "This shit reads like a play. They have typed up what they want me to say. So they want me to testify against Mattie, Lester Bell, and Lenzy Reese? I worked with Mattie at the nursing home, and these two boys have spent the night at my house with my son. As a matter of fact, they are the same age as my son, and they want me to stand up and tell these lies? Oh no! I will not do it!"

"Miss Cooper, if you take the plea, they said that you will not get any more than two to five years, but if you don't, you will get forty to life. And, they said that's a promise."

I said, "They are not God. I can't do that." He said, "Miss Cooper, you're either a fool or you have a lot of faith." I said, "Both. There is a God. I won't do this!" He said, "Okay. I'll them what you said. I'll be back tomorrow." I said, "Alright." He left and the officer came and took me back.

Mattie was standing there looking crazy. She knew just how it felt because the first thing that came out of her mouth was, "Dianne, you know I wouldn't do anything to hurt you." I said, "Mattie what are you talking about?" I didn't have any understanding of anything. This was injustice. I was mad and confused. They tell you what to say and then they take your life. Take you away from your kids. Why? I never sold drugs. I don't know how to sell drugs and all these people know this, but are they standing up for me? No! They are just praying that I don't say anything against them. All they are concerned about is themselves. All of them were drug dealers except me. They all knew how to sell except me. Yet I end up doing the most time. Why? Life isn't fair at all. I went in my room and read that mess my lawyer gave me.

Chapter 9

I couldn't wait for my visit with Shon. I wanted the day to hurry up and be over. I didn't know at the time that Niecy Doll had already taken her plea. She told on Mattie. Dinner came and I went in and read my Bible. I loved to read Psalms. When I got arrested my mama gave me Psalm 71. So I would read it. Then I started reading all the Psalms. That's what I was doing when those ladies from upstairs called themselves going to hurt me. I just kept reading with the door open while they kept talking. Two of them were gay. Both of them were going with the same man and each other.

When I tell you it was some sick females in that jail. They kept leaving and coming back. You could tell the ones who were on crack. They would come in and sleep for two days and when they did get up, they wanted your tray of food and everybody else's. And man, when they use the toilet it is the most sickly, stinking smell. They gain a little weight and then they are gone again. A lot of the girls would come in with those big braids pulled up on their head with the head band. They called them dookey braids. I would buy one of them with commissary and get my hair braided with it. By the time the trial was over, I had a head full of braids.

Now back to the girls talking about beating me up. Do you know they had no reason to feel that way about me? I never bothered them and never said more than two words to any of them, yet they hated me. I never could understand it. When they saw I wasn't going to say anything back, they left me alone. Finally I got up and was headed out the door when Niecy Doll came with a bag of popcorn and her radio talking about, "Dianne, get your radio. My song is on." To be honest, most all of the songs were hers. We would listen to music, look out the window and sing. Niecy Doll was a lot of fun. When she laughed, she made me laugh. Mattie hated it when I was with Niecy Doll, but Niecy was real and down to earth. I could have fun with her. Mattie could never be herself. It was always about what she had and how many cars, the furniture in her house, just bragging all the time. That's not me. I am not into that. That's why I never fit in with her.

That night I just acted silly with Niecy Doll. We did have fun. When she left, I went to bed. I was up early waiting on my visit. We had breakfast and after breakfast, I went to work around 1:00 p.m. They came and got me. When we got to visitation, Shon broke out in a smile and so did I. I said, "What's up, the love of my life." He said, "Hey ma." I said, "Do you know anything about this plea thing?" He said, "Ma, Diamond done told on everybody. They had took him out of jail with us so they could brain wash him. They told him that Humpy had told them everything. Now he done told everything. Ma, we going to prison."

I tried to reassure him. "Shon, if we go we won't do a lot of time. We might have to hit federal ground, but we ain't gonna do a lot of time. You'll see." He said, "I don't know ma." I asked him, "So what's going on with the rest of them, other than being scared?" He said, "They alright. Ma, how cold is that? Diamond believes that Hump would turn on him. I knew they was up to something." I told him, "Yeah, they took Niecy Doll too, and she has already talked on Mattie. Man, this is a mess." He said, "Well ma, we ain't taking nothing, we going to trial. Please don't take that plea. They said if Diamond tell you to take it, you gonna do it."

I said, "Shon, this one thing is for certain and two things are for sure. When it comes between you and your sister, Diamond loses. If you say, don't take it, then I won't take it." He had this big sunshine smile on his face. "I told them you would say that." I said, "I don't understand why most people figure that I would do everything Diamond said." Now, I loved the man and would have done most anything for him, but what a lot of people didn't understand was that I loved my kids more than life. To help or save them, I would do whatever for them. I loved them more than I loved my mama, and she was the queen bee! So I don't know what they took me for.

Shon and my visit ended. He couldn't wait to burst their bubble and I couldn't wait to burst the prosecutor's. When I got back to the pod, I told Mattie about my visit with Shon. She said, "I never did like

Diamond." Well Diamond never did like her either. That's why when she would have her parties he never wanted me to go. But that was between them, it wasn't my fight.

Mattie was scared I was going to take a plea. Most of the time she kept reminding me how she would never do anything to hurt me, but in mind I kept saying to myself, "Yeah and you ain't gonna do anything to help me either." About an hour later, they pulled me out to see Diamond. It looked like every time I turned around they were pulling me out to see Diamond. This time when I saw him I knew something was wrong. I said, "Hey baby what's up?"

He said, "You saw your lawyer, right?"

I said "Yeah, is that what you want?"

He said, "Baby I want you to take the plea. I told them I would explain it to you. Dianne, you can't win. If you take it to trial, you gonna get forty years. Take the plea and all you'll get is two to five. You'll be out in no time."

I said, "Diamond why should I take a plea to something I didn't do? You know I never sold drugs. I can't do that. What about my son, huh? What am I supposed to do about him?"

He said, "I made a deal for Shon, I know how you are about your kids."

I said, "Well me and Shon are going to trial." He couldn't believe it. He thought, like everybody else, that he had more control over me than he really did. Diamond didn't understand. I only allowed him to do what he did because I didn't care. I didn't want to marry him, I was already married and in the middle of divorcing Joseph. I was content with me, him and his other girl, Tamela. Hey, before he got Tamela he was cheating on me. I never saw it. He respected me. He was there for me when I needed him and I respected him and whenever he called I was there, so I was alright.

Nita, my oldest daughter didn't understand that. But I was her mother and she loved me. All she could see was that this man was doing her mama wrong. Man, I love that girl! Anyway, he had no understanding and he said, "Dianne baby, I'm telling you girl, take the plea. If you don't, you going to prison for a long time. Listen to me. When they took me to that jail, they explained to me how it works. See, if you take the deal, you don't have to go to trial. If you don't take the deal, baby I am going to have to take the stand against you. Do you understand what I am saying Dianne? Dianne, baby I don't want to do that. I don't want to hurt you. Tell Shon what I said, alright? Tell him to take the deal."

I looked at him hard. "Alright baby, I'll do what you ask. I won't see him until Thursday. I'm going back in and call home to let them know what's going on." He said, "Alright, tell Linda I said hello." I told him I would. He said, "Dianne?"

I said, "Yeah." He told me to think long and hard about what he just said. I told him, "Baby, why did you take that plea? Humpy ain't told them people nothing. They lied to you."

He just looked at me. "Who told you that?"

"Shon," I said. "Now you think about that." Then they wanted us to leave. The officer said, "Times up." I got up and he was sitting there looking crazy. I went and called Linda and told her about me and Shon's visit and how they keep calling me out to talk to Diamond. Sometimes I get called out three or four times a day. They wanted me to plea bad. I understand now if I would have taken the plea, it would have taken down the key players.

Linda was so upset. She said, "Dianne this is killing madear. I don't think she could take it if you and Shon went to prison. Your girls are catching hell. You and Shon got to beat this. Dianne I am praying. What are Mattie and Niecy Doll doing?" I said, "Disliking each other, but we all have to talk to each other. I'm trying not to get caught in the middle of their little war."

She laughed. "Dianne, I hate you got caught up in this."

"You heard from Leroy?" I asked her.

She said, "Yeah."

I told her not to say anything else because I didn't want know about it.

She said, "I understand."

I said, "If you see him, tell him to watch himself."

She said, "I will."

"Well, sis I'm going to go. I love you."

She said, "I love you too, sis."

I hung up and looked up at the TV and saw one of the girls in here looking at herself on TV. I said, "Damn girl, you did all that?" She started laughing and said, "I guess I did." She and her boyfriend had robbed a bank. I went up to my little room and was sitting there thinking about Leroy. I was remembering one time we were in the club on Oak Street. It was Leroy, Diamond, me and Willie. Leroy came running through the club and this guy was running behind him shooting. I went out the front behind Diamond, while Leroy and the guy went out the back. Diamond and I went behind the car. When Leroy came close enough, I hollered and said, "Leroy, come on." He got behind the car and I pulled my gun out and shot at the guy. He turned and went the other way. I turned and hit Leroy. I said, "Man what the hell have you done now?" They were yelling, "Leroy it ain't over! I'm gonna get you! Your hear me?" Then Diamond said, "Dianne, go inside."

I was as mad at him. He was always getting himself in shit. I left Leroy and Diamond out there talking and I went to get me a beer and played me some music. I sat there laughing to myself. That darn Leroy, I tell you. I got my cup and went to fixing me a cup of black coffee, then went back downstairs to watch TV. A lot of what we watched was news and soaps. Right now, the news was on. I wasn't really paying much attention to the news for real. Mattie's friend Gail was complaining again about being here. I don't know what made her think we liked being in here.

Niecy Doll came over where I was sitting and said, "Hey Dianne, let's go to church tonight. That way we get to see the men." I laughed and thought about it. I said, "Yeah, maybe I'll get to see Shon and Diamond." So we was still watching the news and talking when the officer came in and said, "How many of you want to go to service tonight? All who's going line up right here." So Niecy Doll and I got in the line. Then the officer led us down the hallway single file. We walked past the kitchen. The men were in there and some were mopping. One guy said, "Damn, baby got a nice ass on her." I looked around and Shon was on the man beating and talking to him. Shon was saying "Nigger, you don't be looking at my mama booty, I'll kill ya. You hear me?"

Then officers came from everywhere. I went to screaming, "Leave him alone! Leave my son alone!" The officer who was with us said, "Your son?" I was crying by now saying leave him alone, get off him. I was trying to get to my baby. The lady officer took us into the library and they took Shon and locked him down. One of the men came and got me out of the library and said, "Miss Cooper we didn't hurt your son, we just locked him down. We'll let him out as soon as he cools down. I would have never thought you were his mama. The guy apologized to your son. He said he understood. If a man said that in front of him about his mama, he would have done the same thing. Your son loves you very much." I said, "I love him more. Thank you very much." He said, "No problem."

Chapter 10

After service when we got back, I took a shower and went to bed. Everybody was talking about what had happened. They told me I needed a bigger jumper so I wouldn't upset my son. Man, the new red jumper was so big I had to roll the legs up. Niecy Doll was laughing, she thought it was funny. I didn't at first, and then I had to laugh. My son was something serious. The next day my so called lawyer came. He told me the trial would start next week and it was wrong they didn't give him but two weeks to prepare for his first criminal case. He told me the prosecutor had given him his beeper number and private phone number so he could get in touch with him as soon as I signed the plea.

My lawyer said, "Well they seem to think Diamond can get you to do anything, and believe me he thought the same thing. Well Ms. Cooper, I've got the man who you bought the gun from. He's going to testify on your behalf. You are going to have to help yourself. I need you to dress down. Also you are going to have to take the stand. Are you listening?" I said, "Yes." He said, "Miss. Cooper stop thinking about your son. It won't do him any good if his mother goes to prison." I asked, "How many years did they say he would get if he didn't take the plea?" He said, "Miss Cooper, I am not your son's lawyer. He has his own lawyer."

I said, "Look, I know that. You don't understand. He shouldn't be in here." "Now Miss Cooper, your son has been to jail before. You are the only person who has never been in trouble. If they would give you a separate trial, you probably wouldn't even get convicted. I'm going to do all I can to help you, but I need your cooperation. They are going to have Mr. Edmond speak to you again. Did you read the plea all the way through?"

"Yes," I said. "These people are crazy! How the hell do they expect me to do some shit like that?" The lawyer said, "Miss Cooper calm down. Now I need to ask you something. Do you know where your nephew is?"

I looked at him like he just slapped me. "Why did you ask me that?"

He said, "If you don't take the plea, they want to offer you the same deal if you would just tell them where Leroy Cooper is. Don't say anything right now because you are so upset. Just think about it. I'll be back tomorrow to talk to you. And Miss Cooper, try to focus on yourself and help me help you. Please." Then he got up to leave.

I went back to the pod and went to my room and sat on my bed. I pulled out my Bible and read from Psalms 71. It made me feel better. About an hour later, they pulled me out. It was the detective.

I sat down and said, "Yes?" The detective said, "Miss Cooper why are you being such a hard ass? We got you. I'm sure you know this by now. If you want to see that little daughter of yours grow up and tell us where Mr. Cooper is and we'll see if we can help you out."

I told him, "I see you don't know anything about family. That's my sister's son. It is a thing called loyalty. Do your job cause I ain't tellin you shit."

He got real mean and said, "You black bitch. You gonna die in prison. Come get this black bitch. Get her out of here."

I told him, "Fuck you cracker, you kiss my black ass." While I was saying that, the officer was pulling me out of there. Talk about a red face! His face was blood red. The officer told me while he was taking me back to stop talking to them like that. "You could come up missing." I looked at him and said, "I'm already missing. Haven't you noticed? I'm in jail! I've been going through this shit for a year now."

He said "Oh, no wonder you don't give a damn."

"That's bout right," I told him. He took me back to my pod. I was really sick of this shit for real.

I got on the phone and found out I was a grandmama twice. My daughter had her baby. She had a boy and my son's girlfriend had her baby. She also had a boy. I was so happy. I asked my mama how my baby was and she said Nita was doing fine and so was the baby. Kawanda, my son's girlfriend, was doing good too, and so was the baby. I needed something and being a grandma was it. I hated missing the birth of my grandsons. The worst part was not being there for my daughter… again. I had missed her high school graduation, then her wedding and now the birth of her first child. Lord, I got to get out of this mess. My kids need me.

I got up and went down to see what they were watching on TV. When I got down there, I heard somebody fussing. It was the two girls who had the same man. She caught her girl in the room with one of the girls in the pod. She was mad. I started laughing. I thought to myself, "These are some sick women." Niecy Doll was laughing so hard, she was crying. The more she laughed, the more she made me laugh. We laughed about that for a while. People kept it going and going.

A couple of days later they pulled me out again to see Diamond and like before, I told him no. I was not going along with them. He gave up and they took him out and took me back to the pod. I called Linda and told her to pick me out something to wear to court and we got the officers to let me get a perm for my hair. I had told my sister to just bring me some lipstick, eyeliner and a pair of hoops. We had two days before the trial. My sister had brought Mattie's clothes for her, too.

The night before the trial, the feds pulled me out. I thought we were going to another jail or something. They put me in the car and there was another guy in the back seat. I had never seen him before.

He was just sitting there. The two feds were in the front seat. He and I were behind the glass in the back.

He said, "You don't know me, but I was in the cell with your son last night. You have a nice son. I don't know you, but I heard of you. Diamond used to talk about you. I'm going to have to lie on you tomorrow. You're going to get forty years and I am only going to do five. My name is Jimmy West Taylor. I kill people for a living. If you ever need a favor look me up. I owe you one."

I sat there and looked out the window. I could not believe what that man said to me. What do I do now? I can't take that stand. He just said he was in the cell with my son! After about ten minutes we were back at the detention center. We got out of the car and they took me back to my pod. I didn't talk to anybody. This man was telling me in so many words to keep my mouth shut. I just sat and looked. I didn't know what to do. I had told myself that they were not going to make me cry again and I was staying true to that, so instead of crying, I got mad.

I went to the phone and called my sister. I didn't get an answer so I went down to Niecy Doll's room. We sat in there talking about what we used to do and what we would be doing if we were not in here. She was controlling the conversation. I was just really answering and saying, "Yeah, you're right. Yeah." My mind was a mess. But I wouldn't tell her. She had taken a plea. As far as I was concerned, she belonged to them.

So I sat feeling helpless, wondering how my son was, and wondering what my girls were thinking about me. Later they came and got me out. This was the night before we went to court. Diamond was sitting there. This time we had glass separating us. He said, "Dianne, last chance, baby. Take the plea."

I said, "I told you, I can't."

He shook his head and said, "You gonna get that time."

I said, "I know."

He said, "I got to testify against you. Don't make me do that."

I said, "I wish you well, baby."

He said "See you tomorrow."

I said, "See you, baby."

I went straight to the phone. This time my sister answered. I told her what Diamond said. Then she asked me, "Did you know that Nita used to go with Duck?" I could have fallen through the floor. "Linda what am I going to do? Well sis, I guess I'll see you tomorrow. Oh, what did you bring me to wear?" She said, "Black pants, black suede pumps, and a white blouse. I also got your hoops, lipstick and eyeliner." I thanked her. She said "I'm bringing Alexis with me." I said, "Okay. I hung up. I took my shower and went to bed. At least I thought I was going to bed. Mattie came up and we sat and talked about what was going to happen tomorrow. The trial had everybody a little shaky. Mattie said, "Dianne they gave you a lawyer that never handled a case like this, man." I said, "Yeah. What's your lawyer like?" She said, "He's going to do what he can for me and if we lose, we can always appeal." I told her, "Yeah, well Shon's lawyer said he's gonna try and to what he can for him, too."

Then I asked her, "Hey, is Hattie still over there?" She said, "No they moved her a couple of days ago." I said, "What happened to that Spanish guy who was eating soap? Did he ever come back from the hospital?" She said, "Yeah. I just heard he took a plea. That kitchen boy took one too. They said James fired his lawyer. He's going to represent himself." I laughed and said, "Girl tomorrow is going to be one hell of a day!" She said, "Yeah. Well good night Dianne. I'm going to bed, but I know I'm not going to sleep."

"That makes two of us."

We woke up for breakfast, which none of us wanted. I took my shower and then they took us to the bullpens. The ladies were on one side, men on the other. I was so busy waiting to get a look at Shon that Mattie had to remind me I was supposed to be getting ready to go. I got dressed and was standing over where the men were. I saw Lester, Shon, Lenzy, Tyrone, James, Humpy and Willie. Then the feds came. As we came out, they cuffed us. The men were cuffed and shackled. The ones that cuffed us were two men. One of them was very nice. He said, "Miss Cooper, we'll get you first." I saw he had some gold cuffs hanging on his hip. I said, "Can I wear those gold bracelets?" He laughed. "Sure Miss Cooper, come on," and he cuffed me with them.

After we were all cuffed and shackled, they took us down the steps. Shon and I were riding in the same car. I got in first. When Shon got in he stopped to kiss me on the cheek. And the officer told him, "Hey you can't touch her. Sit down." Shon looked at the man and told him, "That's my mama," and leaned down and kissed me on my cheek. For that second, I felt like a human being, a mother. I looked back at him. He sat right behind me and said, "It's gone be alright ma. We gonna ride this out together." And then he started playing with a piece of my hair.

We rode to the court house. You could see where they had police standing on the rooftops. And the road was blocked off. It was crazy and it really didn't take all that. There were police everywhere. I said, "They got all those feds and police for us? What is wrong with these people?" They took all of us in the back and separated us. The women were in one bull pen and the men in the other. These were different because they were all on the same side. We could all talk to each other, but we could not see each other.

About thirty minutes later they took us in the court room. They had tables with our lawyers standing behind them. I looked at the jury and had a feeling this was not going to be a good thing. They were looking at us like we were already guilty. Shon went to sit by his lawyer. I went and sat by my lawyer and he leaned down and said, "I thought I told you to dress down." I said, "I did." He said, "You look like a drug dealer's girlfriend." I didn't say anything.

The judge came in and we all had to stand and then said his name, the Honorable Judge Alimo. Then we were seated. This man should have not been on the bench. He was about seventy. He had on a neck brace. And he was not paying attention to anything. The prosecutor got up and started talking about the Edmond organization, and me being more than his girlfriend. He said I was his secretary and that I bought the guns for the organization. I could not believe all the lies. This woman, Debbie Stanley drew a whole diagram of Oak Street, while pointing out sections of it. Telling the jurors that this was where Edmond distributed his drugs. Said he ran that town. She went on and on.

Now when they got to James, it was funny. James fired his lawyer and he told the judge he didn't want another lawyer because he was going to defend himself. And he did throughout the whole trial. To be honest, it was a circus. We were the clowns. We didn't have a chance. On day two, I had Linda to bring me a dress. That still wasn't good enough for my lawyer. Oh well, I can only wear what I own. Diamond bought my clothes. While we're waiting, Duck said, "Miss Dianne, I'm sorry. I got to testify against you."

"Well if you sorry about it, why are you doing it?"

"Because they told me to. I took a plea."

Right then I knew I couldn't let Shon take the stand. We all went back in the courtroom and when it came time for Shon to take the stand, I told my lawyer, "Please. I need to talk to my son." When they let us talk, I told Shon, "You can't take the stand." He said, "Ma, I got to defend myself."

I said, "Shon if you take the stand, your sister is going to prison."

He said, "What are you talking about?"

I said, "Nita used to date Duck during the time he killed that woman."

He said, "Man. Okay ma."

So when his lawyer asked him to take the stand, he refused. My lawyer was so mad in the face. Duck lied big time. John John, the killer, had me cooking dope. My cousin, Johnny Bell lied and said I left my job to sell drugs. My cousin Hattie told everything we did the weekend I went to visit her. Down to what brand of cigarettes I bought. She lied, and said I told her to put Diamond's dope in the front of my bag!

The only person who told the truth was the pawn shop owner. He told them how I came in and bought the three guns, a Derringer, a .25 automatic and a .45 caliber. But they said I bought the guns for the organization. To tell the truth, my son paid for the .25 automatic. It was a Christmas present. When Diamond took the stand, they asked him did he know me. He said, "Yes." Then they asked him to point me out and he did. They asked him did he buy me my car. They asked him if he trusted me. He said, "More than he trusted his mother." They asked him did I know what was in that bag that was in my luggage. He didn't say anything. The prosecutor said,

"Remember our deal." Then he looked at me with tears in his eyes and said, "She knew." That was it.

Court was over. It didn't take them long. They took us out and locked us up in the bull pen. While we were waiting, the feds went and bought us some Popeye's Chicken, red beans and rice. I wasn't even hungry. I sat there thinking about that officer who came in my room to pray with me before the trial started. Within three hours they were back. Guilty! Everybody was found guilty. The detectives and prosecutor gave each other a hi-five and said "Yes sah, we got 'em." They looked at us and smiled. During the whole trial, when somebody objected to something, the judge didn't hear them because he was nodding all the time. One time he told my lawyer to "get on with it."

They already knew we were going to prison. When I walked in and looked at those people, I knew I was going to prison. I looked at my baby and my sister. Linda was crying so hard. Alexis didn't know what was going on. When I would look over at her, she would just smile at me. Lord, how I wanted to just go over there and hold Alexis. I wanted to just hold her one last time. To kiss her on her cheek and tell her how much I loved her and how sorry I was for leaving her motherless.

The officer came and took us back to the detention center. They didn't sentence us for about another week. On April 16, 1992, I was sentenced to 480 months! Forty years to life. After the judge sentenced me, he asked me if there was anything I wanted to say. I told him, "Sir, everything they said, I did not do." Then he told the officer to take me back to the bull pen.

When I was walking through, Shon said, "Ma how much time did you get?" I told him 400 and something months. I was so scared for him. They took me back to the jail before I could find out how much time he had. So I asked the officer would he please go around there and ask Benjamin L. Cooper how much time they gave him. He said, "Sure. I'll be right back." So he left. While he was gone I went and made me a cup of coffee. I was just putting it in the microwave when the officer called me to the door and said, "Miss Cooper, he got life." I said, "What did you say?" He said it again, "Your son got life." I cried so hard I almost made myself sick. I didn't come out of there the rest of the night. I was sick.

The next day, Shon and I had a visit. My eyes were swollen. When he saw me he said, "Ma, what's wrong with your eyes?" I looked at him and said, "Boy, the officer told me you had life. I sent him around there to ask you. I never expected that they had given you life. I can't take it baby." He said, "Ma I didn't get life, I got thirty five years." I looked at him and said, "Why did you tell him you had life?" He said, "Because I thought he was trying to get in my business." I said, "Man, don't you ever do that to me again! I almost made myself sick last night worrying about you. I'm thinking you going to die in prison." He started laughing. "I'm sorry ma. If I knew you had sent him, I wouldn't have told him that."

Then I asked about the others. Willie had got life plus forty, Lenzy, Lester and all of them got less than thirty five. He said, "Ma, we ain't going to do all this time are we?" I said, "No, Shon. There is a God. I promise you, we won't be doing all this. I don't know how much of it we got to do, but one thing for sure, we will be going home." I sat back, then I said, "So, daddy Shon, have you talked to Kawanda?" He said, "Yeah. But I haven't told her how much time I got. She's mad because she thought she had given you your first grandchild. Now that she found out about April, she is hot with me." I told him, "I don't blame her." He just laughed, "Ma, we going to be alright." I said, "Yeah baby, we gone be fine." The officer came and told us time up. So they took us back.

I went and called Linda. When she heard my voice she started crying. I said, "What's wrong, Linda? Something happened to madear?" She said, "Girl do you know how much time those people gave you?" I said, "Yeah, 480 months." She said, "Fool that's forty years. Those people gave you forty to life!" I couldn't say anything. For one, it didn't take hold in my mind. I tell you I was not caring about me. I kept thinking about my kids. I said to Linda, "Oh." Then I said, "Damn. Alright sis, stop crying. I am not going to do all that time. Where is madear? How is she doing?"

She told me madear was in the hospital. Now *I* am about to lose it. I said, "What's wrong?" She told me, "When she heard about the time you and Shon got, I guess her blood pressure went up. They had to take her to the hospital. When they took her, we found out she had a stroke. Don't go crazy, Dianne. She's alright." I told her "How can you say she's alright when you just told me she's in the hospital? I am so sorry." She said, "Girl, madear is going to be alright. Don't worry about it."

I said, "How is Nita taking all this?" She didn't say anything for a while, and then she said "Well, you know how she is. She don't talk too much to me. She seems to be closer to Maureen than me these days. So how is Mattie doing?" I told her Mattie was okay. "Right now she's very pissed off at Niecy Doll. You know Niecy Doll helped Mattie get that life sentence. And the truth be told, Mattie is taking it better than I would. Linda, look out for the girls, alright?" She said, "Girl, we're family. Why would you ask me something like that? You know I am going to look out for Nita and Alexis."

I asked her, "So tell me, have you seen Joseph?" She said, "No. I haven't seen him in a while. The last time I saw him, he asked me how you were doing. I told him you were doing alright. He said, 'See Linda, she wanted money, now look what happened. That dope dealer got her in jail with him.'"

I said, "Please. If I would have stayed with him, I would still be in jail. Only it wouldn't be on no drug charges. I would be in here for murder. That fool would have made me kill him. Man, I'm in here getting ready to go to prison. His son's in here getting ready to go to prison. And that's what coming out of his mouth? So many times I wish I hadn't married that man. See Linda, that's one of the reasons we would fight so much."

She asked, "Why?"

I told her, "The stupid shit that comes out of his mouth! I can't believe him. Well sis, I am going to hang up now, my tooth is hurting bad. I'm suppose to go to the dentist tomorrow. Take care, Linda. Love ya."

She said, "I Love you too, baby sis".

I hung up the phone and went and told Mattie that Linda asked about her. I also told her about mama having a stroke, too. I felt like I was killing mama. Mattie said she was going to call Linda later on. We sat and talked about that circus of a trial. Mattie's friend came over. She was crying about the time she had. She said, "I'm going to kill myself." I was so tired of her. I told her, "Do it then. Go ahead and kill your damn self." She got mad at me and left. Mattie said, "Dianne, now why did you do that? She don't mean anything by what she said." I said, "Mattie that woman been complaining and crying since she came here, and at the moment, I really don't want to hear any of what she has to say. She's your friend anyway, not mine." Mattie said, "She pushed herself off on me." I said, "Yeah, right. If you say so."

We looked up and saw her walking with a damn bed sheet. I said, "Mattie look at that damn shit." We walked upstairs where this nut was and Mattie said, "What are you doing?" She said, "I can't take it. I'm going to hang myself." I looked at her and shook my head. I said, "Lady, please. You ain't going to do shit. You just want some attention."

She was crying. I just didn't feel sorry for her. I mean she didn't have any real time. Five years! This woman climbed up on the rail and threw the sheet over the beam and tied the sheet around her neck. I just stood there looking at her. Mattie was standing there telling her not to do it. "You ain't got much time. You going to be alright. Please don't do it."

I looked at Mattie and then said to the girl, "Go ahead, do it. Jump. I don't give a damn. You want it, then jump." Now I really didn't think the lady would do it. But damn if she didn't. That fool jumped! When she did, the sheet popped off the rail and she hit the floor. All that happened to her was that she skinned her neck up and broke her arm. Man, when she landed on the bottom floor my mouth flew open. I couldn't believe she did it! Now did I feel bad? NO! I don't know why, but I just didn't. Officers came running from everywhere. She was lying down there looking dazed. They locked us down for the rest of the night.

I laid on my bed and pulled out my Bible and read Psalm 71. It always made me feel better. I also prayed for mama. And I sat there and talked to God, asking why? I had no understanding about my life. "Lord," I said, "why was I born? Why is all this happening to me? Am I cursed? What is it? Please don't take my mama from me, Lord. Don't take the only parent I have. I need her. I love her so much. Lord, why don't you help me? What have I done so bad that You're letting all this happen to me?" I laid there, getting mad at God for all my trouble.

Chapter 11

The next morning after breakfast, medical called me out to the dentist. I had three teeth pulled at the same time. I had two of my wisdom teeth on one side and one on the other side. He had to cut out two of them. When my feeling came back, talking about pain! I was the first one in pill line. I was getting Tylenol with Codeine and Percodan. The girls were at me for my medication. Niecy Doll was the first one. Those nuts were already smoking banana leaves, greens and now they wanted to crush up my pain pills and smoke them.

But they were in for a rude awakening. I needed my pills. I stayed in pain for over a week before they took the codeine away and started giving me regular Tylenol. When my mouth got better, I started back working in the commissary. On Saturday we cleaned out our room. This particular day, Niecy Doll wanted to buff the floors. She couldn't take up the buffer by herself, so I was helping her.

While we were taking it up the steps, Niecy Doll somehow tripped and fell down the steps. Thank God I caught the buffer, because if I hadn't it would have went right behind her. She hurt her back pretty bad. They came and took her to medical. She was flat on her back for a couple of weeks. Now, I felt bad for Niecy Doll. I saw her fall down those steps. I helped her out for a while by getting her tray in the morning and in the afternoon.

About a week after we were sentenced, Diamond sent the officer to tell me he was leaving and that he was sending his commissary to me. He had a lot of junk food. I saw that his eating habits had changed. Shon sent me a letter and told me the reason they moved Diamond was because all the boys threatened to mess him up. See, when Diamond got to the stand, he told everything. I mean everything. He told who all worked for him and about how long. Now what pissed me off with him was that he said Shon had worked for him off and on. Well, Shon had just got out of boot camp when they arrested him and put him on this case. To me, he had already paid. I couldn't understand how they could come and lock him up. So everybody wanted to hurt Diamond pretty bad.

Right after they moved him, three weeks later they moved Niecy Doll. Hattie never came back after the trial. They started moving each one of us slowly. I starting dreading the day they would move Shon because I knew it would be a very long time before I saw my son again. That day came. They said, "Johnson and Cooper pack up. You're leaving." I asked the officer, "What about Benjamin Cooper?" See, by now they all knew he was my son. He said, "Don't worry, he's packing up too." I thought to myself, good. I get to be closer to him a little longer.

I called Linda to tell her we were leaving. I asked her to come and pick up my clothes from property. She asked where they were taking me. I told her I had no idea. All I knew was that we were leaving this damn place. And I hope never to see it again. Then I asked her how our mother and my girls were. She told me madear was good and she was doing fine. As for my girls, they were having a hard time with me and Shon going to prison. Alexis had already started being rebellious. I told Linda I couldn't blame the child after all she's been through. Then I asked her about Nita. She told me Nita don't say very much. She had a husband and a new baby, so that's keeping her busy. I was glad about that. That helped my guilt trip a lot. I told Linda when I got to where they were taking us, I would call her. She said, "Stay safe." I told her I would then I hung up the phone.

About ten minutes later the officer came and took us down to the first floor. They shackled and handcuffed all of us that went to trial. It was Mattie and her husband, Lenzy, James, Willie, Tyrone, Shon and of course me. They had two vans. I was praying Shon and I rode in the same van. Sure enough, we did. They drove us to Jacksonville, FL to an airfield. Man, when I saw all those guns I almost lost it. I mean everywhere you looked they were standing with those guns up in the air. They parked the van and then called us out, one by one. When we got down, the officers would pat search you and then you would get on the plane. The women sat up front and the men were in the back. We could not turn around and talk to the men. Yet they would call you fine and pretty and say what they wanted. We had to stay facing the front.

I did not like being on that plane shackled and handcuffed. The plane was full of us. The plane was in bad shape, also. Now I was scared. I kept thinking Lord, what if this thing crashes? These people are not going to try and save us. We will all die on this plane, handcuffed. I wasn't the only one scared. Some of the women were crying. I felt like we were a herd of cattle. At that moment I didn't feel like I was human at all. When they had the last inmate on the plane, they had the nerve to tell us to buckle up. How in the hell am I going to buckle up? One of the girls told them she needed help. When I tell you that officer looked at her like she had slapped her. She looked at her so nasty. I wasn't about to ask anyone to help me. The officer helped her, but she let it be known that she didn't want to. I kept on at mine until I got it across me and fastened. Man, this was the pits.

They gave us something to eat. Some cheese crackers, a little juice and a piece of fruit. I didn't drink anything because I didn't want to think about having to go to the bathroom. So I set there and looked out the window and hoped that we made it to where they were taking us all in one piece. That was the longest ride in my life.

We finally landed in Atlanta at Paulding County Jail. I thought the nightmare had ended. I was wrong, it had only just begun. Just when I thought things couldn't get any worse. We stayed in the pit from hell for two days. The next day we rode all day. At dawn they put us in another jail. I didn't know at the time they had taken the men out of Paulding County the day before. I also didn't know that Leroy, my nephew, had turned himself in. He had been in New York all this time. He had taken a plea and was sentenced to ten years.

When the van pulled up, Mattie, myself and two guys that we didn't know got out. We were trying to walk to the door. You know it wasn't easy with those cuffs and shackles. I looked at one of the men and said, "Leroy?" Before I knew it, I had somehow jumped on him. He had caught me. He was smiling so hard and I was too.

Let me explain about Leroy. He was my legal brother. But biologically he was my nephew. I hadn't seen him in over a year. We were raised in the same house. I had missed him so much. So the feds ran to pull us apart. They told us we couldn't talk or touch. Leroy said, "That's my sister." So the officer looked in the file he had in his hand and said, "Give them two minutes." Leroy said, "I was with Shon last night. I spent his birthday with him." I said, "That was right on time. Leroy, what happened?"

"I turned myself in," he said. "Dianne, I am tired." The man said, "Alright let's go," So they put Leroy in the van they had taken us out of. He leaned down and kissed me on the jaw.

We went inside and the lady officer came and got us. She said, "Strip," and sprayed some mess in my hair. I was mad about it. I got in the push button shower. I washed my hair and got out. Then they put us in an orange jumper and took us to a nightmare. The toilet was in the middle of the room with a curtain around it. The bunk beds had no latter. You had to get up and down it the best way you could. Shon sent me a note that said, "If I leave first, I'll send a pack of cigarettes around to you and if you leave first send a pack around to me." We were in this joke of a jail for about two weeks. Shon left first. When the trustee brought me those cigarettes, my heart fell to my feet. I knew it would be a long time before I saw my son again. I was so hurt I couldn't even cry. I just pulled one of the cigarettes out and lit it.

The next day, they came and told us to pack up, we were leaving. When they came to me, for some reason they black boxed me and not Mattie. Black box is a handcuff box. When you put your hands in and try to turn them, the cuffs gets tighter and tighter. And they still handcuffed me. They put us on the plane. It wasn't many of us on it. This wasn't an airlift. This was a plane the government had taken from somebody. I was still in my sentencing clothes and had my braids. Everybody kept looking at me. One girl said, "Why did they black box you? What did you do?" I said, "I chopped up an old man and put him in a garbage bag." That girl moved to another seat. She didn't ask another question. Every now and then I would catch her watching me.

This time one of the female officers buckled us in. I still didn't drink anything on this trip. I just didn't want to have to go to the bathroom. After we were all buckled up, the plane took off. We ended up in California. Mattie and I were taken off the plane. I was thankful when they took that black box off me. Two more officers took over.

They put their handcuffs on us. The feds got their shackles off and the officers put their shackles on us. They helped us in the car and took us to the Pleasanton aka Dublin prison. They took us to R&D, where right off hand the lady told me I had to take the braids out of my head. So I had to go sit in a little room that looked like a big cage with a bench in it and start taking those braids out. Everybody had been processed except me. I had one side of the braids loose, and the other side I was still working on. The officer wouldn't wait. She told me to come on to get my picture taken for my ID card.

I couldn't believe she was going to take my picture with me looking like that. But she did. Oh, I was mad! Man, I looked like a real convict. After she took the picture, a girl named Chocolate came in to be processed. She helped me take the rest of my braids out. She said, "Nice outfit." See, I still had on my court clothes. Black dress pants, suede pumps and so on. I told her thanks. She asked me where I was from. I told her Georgia. She asked me how much time did I get? I told her forty years. She almost dropped the comb.

She said, "Damn! That don't make no sense. You kill somebody?" Finally I laughed and said, "No. I didn't kill anybody."

She said, "Well why so much time?"

I told her, "The hell if I know. I guess they didn't like me."

She said, "Sound more like they hated you." "That's about right." I told her.

We finally got all the braids loose and Chocolate said, "Man, we could make some money on all this hair." When she said that, the officer brought us a trash bag and told us to put the hair in it. So we did. Chocolate went and processed in and then we were taken to laundry to get our bedding, underwear, uniforms, towels and bath clothes. Then we hit the compound. I ran into Mattie again in laundry. When we walked up on the compound, we both stopped. We saw this girl that looked like a boy. I said, "Is this place co-ed?" Chocolate said, "No, girl we missed it by about six months. That's a girl." Later I learned that girls like her were called studs or shims. Junior had a beard and mustache, short and bow legged. I was to meet a lot of "juniors" in the next eighteen years.

Mattie and Chocolate went to the E-F unit and I was taken to A-B unit. The compound was pretty. It looked like a college campus. It was made of brick and glass. This is where my incarceration started. When you walk in, there's the officer's station. It was right in front of you. To my right there was a snack machine and a row of sofas with a TV in front of them, and right before you get to the sofas, there's a pool table. To my left there are rooms with doors. They called this the bus stop. It has three people to a room. There is a wash room and phone booth on every corner you turn. Upstairs they have three-man rooms. In these rooms you have one set of bunks and a single bed. The beds have pull out drawers under them. Downstairs you have the hair room. Each room had a door. You wore the key to your room around your neck. If you lost your key, you had to pay three dollars. You also had the wing rooms which were upstairs, and there are only two people to a room in those. Mostly couples and long timers got those rooms. The only way to get out of the bus stop was for a person to sign a copout saying it was alright for you to move into the room with them. I stayed in A-B unit for about four months. When I moved out of that unit it was such a blessing.

In the bus stop, my roommates was a lady named Laura and this African. Laura was in for killing a baby. She used to shoot up heroine. She was babysitting for some people and had gotten high. She didn't even know she had thrown the baby out of the window until the police woke her up. She had nodded out. I felt sorry for Miss Laura. She would wake us up screaming. Sometimes she said she could hear the baby crying.

My other roommate was forever putting food in the window. It would be so stinky! If we had fish for dinner, she would put it in the window to dry out. My first week there, I was an A&O, so I didn't have to work. I was told I could get a box, meaning I could have some of my own clothes from home. So I called home and told Linda. I said, "Hey girl." She said, "Dianne, hi. Look, I just talked to Shon and he told me he could get a box of clothes. So we're getting his box together. What's going on with you, girl?"

I said, "Girl, I was going to ask about that same thing. Listen I need you to do the same for me. From what I understand, I can have four pairs of earrings, one gold chain, a watch, one wedding band, one of pair pumps, a pair of tennis shoes, a pair of bedroom shoes, one robe, one sweater, seven pair of panties, seven bras, four pair of jeans, four shirts, one slip, one dress, four pairs of socks, one pair of stockings and one pair of pajamas." She said, "Alright send me the papers and baby sis, I will hook you up. So how are you doing?"

"I'm okay," I said. "Girl, this place is something else. They got gang bangers in here. There are different races and colors in here. I ain't lying. Mattie lives in a different unit, so I mostly stay to myself. Hey while you getting that box together, send some funds alright? I need some money."

She said, "Speaking of money, Diamond just sent me some money to send to you."

I said "What? What do you mean he sent you some money to send me?" Linda said, "Just what I said. He sent me some money to give to you. So you will be getting some money once a month from Diamond."

I said, "So he gets me locked up with him and sends me some money. Oh that's just great."

"Calm down, Dianne. It's going to work out. Look, let's get your stuff together, alright?"

I said, "Yeah. Did Shon say anything else other than about the clothes?"

"Yeah, he said when I walked onto that compound, ma's words came to me. She said boy, one of these days you going to get yourself into something I won't be able to get you out of. I knew I had to become a man. I was on my own."

I got upset. "Oh, Linda! Why did they send my child to a USP penitentiary, a damn penitentiary? He's only twenty one years old."

Linda said, "But he's not by himself. He has Lenzy and Lester with him."

"Yeah, I am happy about that." Linda told me that he had written me. I told her I love her and hung up. I stood there feeling helpless. Then I got mad! I went to the track, and when I got there I let God have it! I was so mad. I asked God, "What kind of God would send a twenty year old child to a penitentiary where he could get killed? You let that judge give him thirty five years! Why are You taking his youth? And You might as well kill me. You done took my whole life. GOD! Where is this loving God I keep hearing about? Where is Your love for us, huh? Who the hell are You? Why did You let this happen? Huh? What are You about? What? You just sit up there and play with people's lives!

I was crying so hard I couldn't see. I raged on. Why did You create me? Huh? If this is it, then I don't want it. I walked and cried. I was mad, hurt and pissed off with God! By the time I left that track I had made up my mind. I was going to investigate God. I was going to find out all there was about Him. There was a reason why He let this happen. I mean, I didn't sell drugs, yet He separated me from my world. My everything! And I'm going to find out why! I mean who does He think He is? Well I am going to find out. I went to the library and found every book I could on angels, prayers and Jesus. At the time, I didn't understand that all I had to do was read the Bible. I was on a mission. I had to find out what kind of God would let this happen. That would hurt my child like this. I felt like He had something against me.

When I had calmed down, I went to my unit to watch TV. I loved lying on the couch watching TV, but sometimes I could get an attitude because I can hear the pool balls clicking and girls would be making all kind of noise, laughing and such. During times like that I would get up and go to my room. A couple of months later, I was watching TV when my counselor called me to his office and asked me if I wanted to be in the drug program. I asked him what kind of benefits would I get. He said, "Miss Cooper, does it always have to be something in it for you?" I said, "Yes." He said, "It's a year long program and it's new. Once you finish, you get a year off your sentence and a year aftercare. You also have to make it over to C-D unit. Are you interested?" I told him, "Sure, I ain't got nothing but time. A year off isn't helping me much, but hell I'll take it. By the way, why is it that C-D unit has carpet and no other unit does?" He said, "Well Amy Fisher was in that unit and her father wanted her to be comfortable and the only thing the government would let him do was put carpet in the unit, nothing more." I said, "Oh. Well when do I move?" He said, "Tomorrow when you get off work." I said, "Cool.

Anything else?"

"No Miss Cooper, nothing else." I left his office and went to my room and told Miss Laura that I was moving tomorrow to the C-D unit and that I was going to do the drug program. She said "I'm going to miss you Dianne." Over time, I became very fond of Miss Laura. I told her, "I am going to miss you too." She asked me, "What's for dinner?" I said, "I don't know." She said, "For somebody that works in the kitchen, you don't ever know what's on the menu." "Miss Laura," I said, "I work in the dish room and I'm not a cook."

In the kitchen they had the diet line and the regular line. You could eat inside or out on the patio. Most smokers like me ate out on the patio. The girls that worked in the kitchen made a lot of money stealing. We had many customers that would like tomatoes, onions, chicken, shrimp, sugar, flour, and most of the time I wouldn't have to go to the store. I would just give out a list.

Many of the girls had girlfriends of their own. This enabled me to make a good amount of money supplying them with wedding cakes. They would pay fifty dollars for items like that all the time. Believe me, it wasn't easy getting stuff like that out of the kitchen. That's why you always had a partner. On the wedding cakes, they were sheet cakes and we would put one sheet cake in front of you and one in back. We would bring the icing in our bra to the unit. As for the chicken, we would put a case in a black trash bag and hide it on the patio. Afterwards we would have somebody who worked the day shift to pick it up on their way to the unit. If you got caught in the kitchen, the foreman was going to give you hell.

Our foreman was cool. One time, one of the girls had stolen some shrimp. The cook foreman came in the unit and while walking up the steps started hollering, "Bitch, give me my damn shrimp. I done told you bitches about stealing from the kitchen before I cook my menu." He came back down with a cooler of shrimp. The next day they fought in the cage. The cage is the storage place where we keep the flour and dry goods. If you get into a fight in the kitchen or got caught stealing, they would send you to the SHU (Solitary Housing Unit). Instead, the cook foreman would take you to the cage and you and the foreman would fight. I had to fight him one time. It was when I was working the dish room windows.

See, everyday this girl would sling her tray through the window and I'd ask her to please not sling the tray because when she did, food and water would get all over me. She kept doing it. This day was not the day. I had found out that my son was in the SHU and she came and threw it again. She slung that tray and I snatched her right through the dish room window and slung her into the darn dish machine. I was trying to run her ass through the dishes while I punched her and talked to her. My foreman came in after hearing the girls holler "Fight!" He said, "Cooper, no!" I had her riding with the plates down in the machine. He snatched me back and then pulled her off the dish machine.

He said, "You crazy, bitch. You're trying to kill her!" I said, "Hell yeah, I told that stupid bitch to stop slanging the damn tray through the window." I went at her again and he sent her to medical and sent me to the cage to lock me in it. I was cursing him out and he kept saying, "Alright Cooper, that's enough. Shut the hell up." I was on a roll. I said, "Man, fuck you. Who the hell do you think you are? I ain't scared of you!" He said, "That's enough!" I told him, "What are you going to do, huh?" He knocked the hell out of me and then we went at it! When we were done, I had flour all over me and a busted lip. He said, "Now chill out, Cooper." He helped me up, and then locked me in the cage. I stayed locked up in there until it was time for me to get off from work.

The girl that kept slinging her tray at me told medical she fell over some weights at the weight pile. I was out the next day. When I moved into the C-D unit, I had a problem with this other girl. I was coming from shopping one day and this girl was standing by the door of my unit. She said, "Hey Cooper, I got something for you."

I said, "Who are you and what could you have for me?"

She was looking at me funny and said, "A bag of commissary. This."

I looked at her like she was crazy. "Oh child, you got me confused with somebody else.

She said, "No I don't. Ain't your name Dianne Cooper? And you don't you have a forty to life sentence?"

I said, "Who told you all my business?"

She said, "Don't worry about it."

I said, "I'm not worried, but you may as well take that back to your unit cause I ain't gay," and went to my room. My roommate Lupy said, "Dianne what's wrong?" I said, "Nothing I can't handle."

I got up to put my commissary into my locker and to call me a place in the shower. That was the first time I noticed an officer coming out of the shower with Janice. I stopped dead in my tracks and said, "What the hell is this?" The officer said, "You new around here, aren't you?" I said, "Yes." He said, "How much time do you have?" I told him forty years. He said, "First lesson, mind your own damn business and you'll never see nothing, understand?" I said, "Yes."

"What's your name?"

"Cooper."

He said, "I'm going to remember you, Cooper. If you learn to do time properly, I'll be seeing you." He started to walk off then stopped, turned around and said, "You work in the kitchen because I remember the foreman talking about a Cooper who threw good left hooks. You that Cooper?" I said, "I don't know what you talking about, sir." He smiled and said, "Very good, Cooper. I like you already," and walked off.

I stood there thinking to myself, what just happened? I know I didn't just have a conversation with an officer who just came out the shower with an inmate. I turned around and went back to my room.

Lupy already knew something was wrong. She said, "Did you call a spot for the shower?" I said, "No. Janice was coming out. I came to get my shower bag and gown." She looked at the clock and burst out laughing. I said, "What's so funny? What's wrong with you?" She said "You saw Janice and the officer? You ain't got to answer me, I can tell. If you don't want to be bothered don't ever take a shower at 9:00 p.m. If you do, he's going to walk right in on you. He always brings an extra uniform to work." I said, "Girl stop lying." She said, "Yeah, he'd love to get you. He won't bother me. I'm not his flavor. He likes Africans and black girls." I said, "But he's a blue-eyed blond." She said, "Yeah. His son's mama is black." I thanked her for the warning.

I went and took my shower and came back. I put on some sweats and went back outside to sit on the bench to smoke and think. I loved sitting there. While I was sitting, chilling, here comes this girl again. "Hey Coop. Look, now be serious. All that time you got, you might as well get with the program. If you're not gay yet, you will be. I mean, come on girl. Forty years!" I said, "Look, find you somebody else and leave me alone. I told you I am not gay and I will never be gay. I don't do, nor will I ever do women." I threw my cigarette down and went to walk off when the crazy girl grabbed me and said, "Look bitch, you're going to be mine whether you want to or not. Like I said bitch, get with the program."

I was trying to get loose from this big bear when another girl came up and said, "What's up Tina?" She said, "Nothing." I said, "Look, turn me a loose and leave me alone, I told you. Just leave me the hell alone!" The other girl said, "Tina, leave that damn woman alone. You always trying to force your big ass on somebody. You give gay women a bad name." Tina turned me loose and told the girl, "Fuck you." She said, "You wish," and started laughing.

She turned to me and said, "What's your name?" I said, "Dianne Cooper." She said, "Nice to meet you, Dianne. I'm Theresa. Everybody calls me Reecy. So you haven't been here long have you?" I said, "No, just a few months." She said, "Girl, you got a lot to learn. If I were you, I would perm my hair and get me some makeup. See Dianne, the reason Tina and a few more want you is because you look like a shim. You got your hair braided back. You don't wear makeup and that walk you got. You stroll. So if you want to get the heat off you, you need to change your look. And if it makes you feel safer, tell them you're my woman and they won't bother you. Everyone thinks I'm crazy." I laughed and said, "Thank you Reecy." She said, "Why are you here, Dianne? You don't belong here. Don't let this place steal who you are. Hold on to yourself. See you later."

I went back to my room and my other roommate, Jenna was in there. She said, "What's up, Bunkie." I said, "Oh nothing, except I got this crazy woman, Tina, chasing me. Trying to turn me gay. If it wasn't for Reecy we would have ended up fighting. And to tell you the truth Jenna, she might have beat me down because that's a big girl." Jenna said, "Oh no Bunkie, she wouldn't have beat you, she would have found a way to rape you, but now you don't have to worry. She won't bother you now. Bunkie, you need to stop looking like a boy."

I said, "I don't look like a boy, I just got my hair braided back and no makeup."

She said, "Did you wear makeup at home?"

I said, "Yeah, every day, and kept my hair up."

"So why you don't do it here?"

I said, "For what?"

"For you."

I thought about that, then I told her, "You are the second person who's told me that today. Tomorrow I am perming my hair, because I am tired of people trying to make me something I'm not." She laughed at me and said, "So when you start your drug class?" I told her, "Next week. They still ain't through with the building. "Oh," she said. Then she told me she was leaving. She was transferring to Lexington. I told her I was going to miss her. Lupy was going home next week.

I went upstairs to the TV room to watch a little news. While I was there Belinda came. She said, "Coop what's up?" I said, "Nothing. What's up with you?" She said she had a new girl friend that just got here. Belinda was in for bank robbery. She didn't get but ten years. The lady was crazy. We had another one that worked landscapes. She couldn't go home until President Ford died. I felt sorry for her because she was truly a very sweet lady. She never bothered anyone. All she wanted was for Ford to die so she could go home. Then there was Red, one of the Helter Skelter girls. She still thought she was a flower child. That man still had mind control over her.

The Spanish mamas ran the compound. Now these two got what they wanted, when they wanted it. For one thing, our warden was a whore. You could always tell who was going with the warden because she would have on red underwear. All his girlfriends wore red underwear. One night we were getting dressed to go to the barn. I had ironed my jeans and blouse. I was trying to decide if I was going to wear my flats or boots. Belinda came downstairs to ask me if I wanted to go to the movies with them. I told her no, I was going to the dance. So she said, "Coop, you got any weed?" I told her, "No, but Angela does." She said, "Now you know she don't like me. She'll give you one." I looked at her and said, "You knew that shit. That's why you came in here. Look, I got one joint. Meet me at the weight pile in about twenty minutes and I want a drink of that liquor, too. I know that ain't water in that cup, bitch. You hate water." She laughed and said, "Are you sure you ain't from California, because you don't act like you from Georgia."

"Well how do Georgia people act?"

She said, "Like your high class co-defendant."

I said, "Lady, get a life. That's just Mattie. Nobody acts like that but her. Don't pay that no mind. Now get out, I got to put my face on."

She said, "Your face is on ain't it?"

"No!" I said, laughing. "I'm talking about my makeup, girl. You know Top Cat from the radio station is coming. I hope to get a dance with him. And if not with him, then his friend. You females get on my nerves. A woman knows what another woman wants. Bull! A woman never had anything for another woman. Look at you and your girlfriend, you two fight like me and my ex-husband. There is no way in hell I would have a woman telling me what to do, other than my mama. What can she do for me? Nothing! When you grow another leg, holler at me okay!" She laughed, "Oh fuck you Cooper! I'll see you in fifteen minutes." I said, "Hey don't forget I want my portion out of your cup, too."

Belinda left and I finished getting dressed. I ended up wearing my black flats. I grabbed my cup, went to the ice machine to put some ice in it and that's when I saw the officer again, the one that was in the shower with Janice. He said, "Well hello Miss Cooper. It is Cooper right?"

"Yes, it's Cooper."

"Miss Cooper where are you in such a rush to go?"

"To the barn."

He said, "I would think you would be off to the movies to steal a little time in the dark with your girlfriend." I got mad, but didn't show it. I said, "I don't do women. Men only, sir." He laughed and said, "And how much time do you have? Forty years? You might not do a woman, as you put it now, but you will." I got real mad and said, "I can always turn into a whore and ride out my time fucking officers like you!"

He turned red in the face first, then gave me a slow smile and said, "Cooper I like the way you think. I'll be seeing you." I told him," I just bet you will, sir." I went and got my ice.

My heart was beating so fast I just knew it was going to come out of my chest. I was thinking, now Dianne why did you say that? Now you're in trouble. You don't even like white men. Shit! I walked out the door speaking to people along the way, walking fast, trying to get to the weight pile so I can get high and a little drunk. Then I wouldn't think so much. As I passed the girls, I was looking at these outfits. These ladies were clean! Some had on pumps and jeans. Others had on their dresses.

Now about the barn, we called it the barn because that's what it looked like, a big white barn. Inside was a gym and a big basket ball court. In there we skated and had dances. On the weekends, Top Cat, a black guy with long dread locks, came. We call him Top Cat because he wears a black top hat. His friend is a nice looking caramel-colored young guy. Belinda was there and so were a lot of other girls. Everybody was getting their high on. Belinda poured me some liquor in my cup. She said, "Girl you going to drink that raw?" I said, "Yeah." She said, "Coop, girl don't you need to pour some coke or something on that? Girl that's hundred proof." I said, "Good, that's even better." While I lit a joint, Belinda said, "Coop don't get caught high. You know if you do, you going to bring heat down on everybody."

I said, "I know where I am. Do I look like I got stupid written on my forehead? Fool, I'm getting high because of where I am. Stop tripping on me. You just don't get caught in no 205 having sex with another inmate." She laughed. "Well that's one thing you don't have to worry about, now ain't it?"

"You got that right, girl friend." I said, "Man, I don't see how you do that shit. While you got me talking, pass that joint. You ain't slick." She hit it again and told me, "See you later, sister." I told her, "Yeah. Have fun." I smoked the rest of my joint and put the roach in my cigarette pack and tried to remind myself to flush it when I go to the bathroom. When I finished my cup of liquor, I chewed a piece of garlic and then popped a peppermint behind it. Lit another cigarette, smoked it and went toward the barn.

Mr. Bowlegged Jones was at the door. He's a cool black officer. When I walked in, we spoke and then I moved on. I was trying to focus to see if I could spot anyone I know. I spotted Tina and her new woman. After Tina heard about my fight in the kitchen, I got new respect. Nobody bothered me. And I still had Reecey on my side. I spotted Mattie and her clique. I moved close as I could to the DJ. I did get me a dance that night. He danced with about four of us at the same time.

They called compound closed at 9:45. Everybody went back to their unit. The movie was over. You saw couples in corners and behind trees trying to get that last good night kiss. There were a lot of pregnant girls over from when it was co-ed, men and women in prison. Gloria Ann used to tell me some stories about how the officers would pay an inmate to clam up because the husband and wife would end up on the same compound. But before the husband came on the compound to be with his wife, he had been on the down low. And the boyfriend would get jealous of the wife and tell on him. The husband and boyfriends were going together at the last prison. I would laugh so hard at that girl. She's pregnant for an officer right now. But he didn't do that with her. He was claiming his baby. She should have it in a couple of months. I asked her were they going to be together. She said she didn't know. I wish her the best. She's good people.

I went on to my unit and laid out my shower bag and grabbed my PJ's and waited on them to count. While I waited, Renda Taylor came to my door and said, "Cooper when do your roommate leave?" I said, "In a couple of weeks, why?" She said, "Pat wants to move in with you. She told me to ask you." I said, "Who the hell is Pat?"

She said, "I'll show her to you after count." I said, "Alright. I'm going to take a shower first, and then I'll come down to your room, okay?" She said, "Alright. Hey Coop, you got coffee?" I said, "Yeah." She asked me to bring her some. I told her I would. It took them forever to count us. During those days I would always take my shower after count. I did not want that officer walking in on me. After count I went down to Renda's room. Now you talking about a trip, Renda was that. One moment she was all about the Bible and the next she would be walking around with her robe open, showing her body. She wouldn't have anything on, just the robe. Other than that nasty habit she was real good people.

I went down there and she was telling me about this girl named Pat. She said Pat and I would get along. She said Pat was laid back and cool. I told her I would sign the copout for Pat to move in when my roommate left. So that Monday, she left. Lupy asked me, "Why is it you won't let anyone love you? You always push people back." I told her, "I don't understand what you're talking about."

She said, "Like us. I love you very much. We could be sisters. But as soon as we started becoming friends, you pushed me back. Coop, you are going to have to trust somebody." I told her, "I do trust somebody, my mama who birthed me and my kids whom I birthed and my sisters." She just shook her head and said, "Coop those people ain't in here with you." I told her, "They are always with me," and I walked off and left her standing there.

I went to the lobby and got me a soda and a pack of Famous Amos Cookies, found me a spot on the sofa and watched a little TV. I wanted to stay out there until Lupy went to sleep because I didn't want to hear what she was talking about. I was deep into a movie when something hit the sofa I was sitting on. I looked and there was a half a pint of vodka. I looked up, and smiling at me was the officer who was with Janice in the shower. I put my vodka in my pants before anybody noticed. He was walking to the officer's station and I was sitting there, looking stupid. I started thinking, "Dianne girl, this is the police who just threw a half a pint of vodka to you. Now he's not giving you this for nothing." Oh well, I'll worry about it later. Right now I need to hide this until the weekend.

So I got up and went to my room. The door was locked, so I took my key from around my neck and opened the door. Lupy was in her bed sleep and my other roommate was facing the wall. So I took it as her being asleep. I pulled the bottle out of my pants and put it in my pillow. "I'll sleep on it tonight," I said to myself. "I'll take it to work with me and hide it in a sack of flour." So that morning when the officer woke me up at three thirty a.m. to go to work, I got up. I never cut on a light. I learned to dress and put on makeup in the dark.

Both my roommates worked at Unicore and I didn't want to cut the light on while they were still sleep. So I did everything in the dark. When I finished getting dressed, I went out front with the rest of the kitchen workers, got counted and went across the compound with the half of pint of liquor in my bra. When I got to work I went to check the menu to see if we were having anything that needed flour before the weekend. We were having pancakes Thursday and biscuits on Friday. I saw that we were not having grits anymore that week. I went and put my liquor in the grits for safe keeping until Friday.

With that taken care of, I was off to the dish room to find Belinda. She was putting dishes in the machine that the workers used. She looked up and said, "What up Coop? Girl you need some coffee. You don't look like you're awake yet." I told her, "Nah I am wide awake. I just got a lot on my mind. So what's up with you?" She said, "Oh same old thing, just waiting on the weekend. Cooper girl, I am so tired of prison, I don't know what to do. Now all I do is live for the weekend, and wish for a cool officer so we can do what we want to do." I told her, "Yeah, let's get this day over with." She said, "Hey, doesn't your roommate leave today?" I told her, "Yeah." Then she asked me, "So Coop, you already got somebody picked put to be your new roommate?" I said "No why?" She said, "No reason, just asked." I didn't tell her about Pat. I had learned to watch what I said to her. She was alright with me, but her girl was a whole different thing. I didn't talk around her like that. She and I made it through the day.

When I got off from work, I jumped in my sweats and went to the weight pile and track. I would stay out there until about three, and then go in to beat Unicore's rush. If I go in at three, I can get my shower and iron. Then I'm out of everybody's way. While they are fussing over the iron and shower, I can chill. That's why I loved my good government job in the kitchen. I went to work while everybody was asleep and I was off from work while everybody else was working.

I didn't make any money. Twelve cents an hour and got paid once a month. On payday I made eighteen dollars. I was lucky. But hey, I wasn't wanting for anything. Reason being, I was learning how to get my hustle on. The first thing I was going to hustle up was some perfume oil bottles. I was going to wash them out and sell liquor. I believe three dollars a bottle might be about right and with that half pint, I should make out pretty good. Shoot, I just might be onto something here. Yeah, I am going to be alright in here. I just got to figure out how to make the system work for me.

Chapter 12

Well, Pat moved in with me. When she moved in, my other roommate moved out. The reason she moved out was she learned that Pat was gay. I guess she thought Pat was going to rape her or something. I mean come on, half the prison population was gay or bisexual. So you might as well deal with it. Pat and I became fast friends. We learned to respect each other as a person. Her being gay had nothing to do with the person she was. She respected me because she said I had integrity. And she thought it was cool how I got along with the officers.

See, I learned to work with them. I would look out for them. If they were in one of the girls' room getting their groove on, I would look out for them. Like I said, when Janice and her officer was in her room, I would sit in the lobby and watch TV. If I saw another officer coming, I would go knock on the door and let her know either the police was coming or her roommate. She didn't trust her roommate. She had a key to their room, but if you stuck your toothbrush in the door, the key wouldn't turn. That went for the staff keys also.

I kept liquor. Sometimes I would trade liquor for weed. It worked out good for me. Now my roommate was something serious. She had a girlfriend in A-B unit and one in E-F unit. We fell out for a minute because one Saturday I woke up and she had one of her girlfriends in the room. I was mad at her. I just laid there until her girl left and then told her, "Now Pat, what you do is your business, but I be damned if you are going to be having sex while I am in the room. I don't want to hear or see that shit. Damn man, why did you do that?" She said, "I don't know Coop, I'm sorry. It won't happen again. She wasn't supposed to be over here anyway." I said, "What do you mean, she ain't supposed to be over here?"

Pat said, "She's my girl from E-F. She wasn't supposed to come over until after four o'clock count." I told her, Girl you need a lil black book so you can keep track of your women. You can know the time when each one comes and then that way, I would know to be out of the room." I said, "Hey Pat, that's what I'll do. I'm going to the commissary and buy one of those phone books and you tell me when you want to go get your girl. I'll be out here on the sofa watching so you won't get caught. When that one leaves, I'll go get the other one for you. And then they go shop for you. You just get me something. What you think?" She burst out laughing and said, "Coop the pimp," and then she laughed again and said, "I love it friend. I think you are on to something. I needed to be your roommate a long time ago." Then she said, "Coop, I am sorry about my girl in the room and us having sex while you were in there. It won't happen again." I told her I knew she was sorry. So our plan worked beautifully. I never had to buy anything from the store. Pat had it going on.

One day she came to the room with this blonde girl. She was a nice looking girl. Pat said, "Coop, meet Lena AKA Rolex Queen." I had heard about the Rolex Queen. I said, "Hey how you doing?" She said, "I'm good." I didn't answer, I just told Pat I had to make a quick run, and I'd see her later. I went to find Belinda. She was at the pool table shooting a game with her new girlfriend. Belinda changes girlfriends faster than you can change underwear. She can't keep a girlfriend because she likes to beat on them. I don't understand how they let that short, round woman beat on them like that. I think they like it. Anyway, I needed to see Belinda about my money! She hadn't paid me for her bottle of vodka.

See that's why I didn't want to sell her one because she and I are alright. She felt like I shouldn't charge her. Wrong answer! One thing I learned from my ex-boyfriend was that business was business, and bullshit was bullshit. So if she thinks she's going to get away, well she's not. I waited until she finished her shot and said, "Belinda can I holler at you?" She said, "Yeah, what's up Coop?" I said, "Belinda can I get that from you? I'm kind of low in cigarettes." She "Oh yeah, I almost forgot. Look, I'm going tomorrow, come by my room later. You know you didn't have to run me down. I was going to handle my business."

I said, "On whose time? Yours or mine? Just like I gave it to you, you should have come back at me the same way. But no problem, we straight, right?"

"Yeah right."

"See you later then."

I left and went outside, lit me a cigarette and started thinking about home. Wondering what everybody was doing and wishing I was anywhere but where I was. I finished my cigarette and went back inside and walked down to my room. Ms. Rolex Queen, her friend and Pat was in there talking. When I walked, in all eyes fell on me. Ms. Rolex said, "Um, Coop, is that what they call you?" I looked at her and said, "Yeah and why?" She said, "Pat tells me that you've never been with a woman, is that true?" I said, "What's that to you and why are you asking me that?" Pat started laughing. I looked at her, then climbed up on my bed. I was sitting up there when she came with that question again.

"Coop, have you been with a woman?"

I said, "What is it to you? Are you writing a book on me or something?" She said, "No and why don't you just answer the question?"

I screamed, "NO! I've never even thought about it, alright?"

She said, "You don't know what you're missing, girl. Come on and let us show you."

I looked at her and said, "Lady, if you want to live to see tomorrow, don't come up in here fucking with me. Pat, do something with your girl."

But all she did was laugh. That girl came up on my bed and I jumped down and said, "Girl, you better leave me alone! What the hell is wrong with you?" She grabbed my arm and said, "Come on, Coop. You'll like it." I snatched away from her and ran out the room. Damn if she and her friend didn't come behind me! I ran up to Belinda's room and they were still behind me. I got behind Belinda and said, "Belinda help me out. That stupid bitch is trying to turn me out." Belinda started laughing. She said, "Shit, she can turn me out anytime."

I ran a circle around Belinda and ran down to Renda's room. Her door was open. I said, "Renda!" I was out of breath almost. She said, "What are you all doing? Running around the unit?" I ran behind her and said, "I am running from these crazy whores. Help me!" The girls were still behind me. Renda asked them, "What the hell are you trying to do to her?" Ms. Rolex Queen said, "Trying to show her what she's missing." Renda said, "I'll show you what you're missing. Get the hell out of my room and leave this woman alone. It's almost ten o'clock count. Get out!"

Then Renda asked me what happened. I told her all about when I walked into the room and how my bunkie was just laughing, like it was a big joke. She said, "Well, as you see, I don't have a roommate. If you want, you can move in with me. I won't do like Pat and let them rape you. Come on, Coop. It's going to be okay. First thing tomorrow morning, I'll do a copout. I'll walk you to your room. After count, come back down here."

So she walked me to my room and went back to hers. Pat was sitting on her bed and said, "Coop I didn't know they were serious. I thought they was playing. I'm sorry. The only reason I knew they was for real was when Renda ran them out of her room. They came and told me." I said, "You know what, Pat? Kiss my ass. You know, it was like you wanted them to do it. Well, tomorrow I'm moving and if your little friends bring their asses back in here, I ain't running all over the place like no punk. I am going to fuck somebody up. Now let them try me." I had stop crying, I was mad as hell. I was mad I had let them make me cry.

When count was over, I was sitting on my bed with a lock in my sock and a razor blade in a toothbrush. They came back in the room and said, "Hey Coop. You decided to give in?" Pat said, "If you two want to see tomorrow, I suggest you leave Coop alone. The lady is ready to kill all us. There isn't a gay bone in her body. She has integrity. Leave my damn bunkie alone. Come on let's go shoot a game of pool." Then Pat turned back to me. "Coop, I am sorry. Please don't move. I know you. You planning on moving, ain't you?" All I said to her was "Please stop talking to me and get out of my face." She left out. I stayed woke until she came back in to go to bed. When I was in bed, I put the razor and lock under my pillow and went to sleep.

The next morning after work, I went and found Renda and we took a copout to the counselor and I moved in her room. When Pat got off from work, I was gone. At work I didn't have much to say to Belinda. I told her just pay me and we were going to leave it at that. She said, "Girl I thought you was playing. I didn't know you was for real. Come on Coop, I'm sorry." I told her, "Look just leave me the hell alone. All you sick ass gay motherfuckers." She walked off.

We didn't deal with each other after that. She would send other people to get a bottle of vodka from me. One of the officers I be penning for asked me was there some girls trying to rape me. I told him no. I asked him, "Who told you that lie?" He answered, "It doesn't matter since it's a lie. Which I know it isn't a lie, but Cooper I have much respect for you. Watch yourself okay? Lady, there are not many like you around here."

I was heading toward the laundry room when two bloods (gang members) stopped me and said, "Hey, go stand where you can see the officer's station and let us know when he's coming." So I went a few feet back the way I came. I saw the officer. He was at the officer's station. The girls went in a room and I heard a girl holler and a lot of stomping. It didn't last five minutes. Then the girl said, "Thanks," and went back up the hall. I walked down where they were coming from and it was this white girl lying on the floor. She was in the fetal position. Her face was bloody. I looked at her and took off to the track. I didn't want to be in the unit when they found her.

Sure enough I saw the officer running toward the unit and medical. So I knew they had found her on the floor. The two that had beaten her was at the weight pile working out like they hadn't done anything. I just kept walking and saying "Lord, I don't belong here. Why am I here? I don't belong here."

After all that had happened, I settled into Renda's room. Nobody wanted to live with Renda because she stayed naked, like I told you before. One minute she is all into the Bible and the next minute she's trying to turn you out. In other words, get you to have sex. I used to laugh at her. She would come in and take off her clothes, put her robe on and leave it open. I use to say, "Roommate, put some clothes on or close your robe. You are not turning me on. You are turning me off." That was her downfall. Her husband was younger than her. She was good people. She had ten years for bank robbery. Her husband thought it was still co-ed, so he went and robbed a bank because he thought he would end up with her. When she told me about that, I laughed until I cried.

How about her and the Bible? Renda knew the Word. She had over a hundred Bible certificates. It was like this one Bible she had. Oh, I loved it! I had asked her where she got it from. She told me a church had sent it to her. It was about seven days before my birthday. I got off from work and the Bible was on my bed, along with a picture of her in the back of it. She touched my heart then. We became very good friends. When she walked with her robe open she would have on a bra and a pair of shorts. I thanked her for that.

She and this one officer were tight. One night before count I had my hair in a lot of braids. He came into Renda's room and was joking around with her. Then he looked at me and said, "Who is this? You got a roommate?" She said, "Yeah man, that's Cooper. She's good people." In other words, that's Cooper: she don't tell nothing. She keeps her mouth shut. He said, "Is that so Cooper? How long have you been down?" I said, "Six and a half months."

"How much time you got?"

"Too much."

"How much?"

I didn't want to tell him how much for real. I went on and told him forty years.

"Damn, girl! How many people did you kill?"

I said, "I didn't kill anybody. I just wouldn't help them."

He said, "I don't know what to say, except stay out of trouble. Gotta go." When he left out Renda said, "Man Coop, they dogged you. Ain't no reason for them to give you all that time."

"Yeah well, I ain't gone do all that time anyway. Hey, you know that five hundred hour drug class I'm in?" She said, "Yeah." I said, "How about they were so in a hurry to throw that building up, they didn't put the inmate bathroom in. So if you have to go to the bathroom, you have to go to your unit. And that Dr. Johnson, he gets mad at me in our one on one session. He said I must learn to communicate. Renda, I do communicate. He supposed to be talking to me about my drug problem." She said, "Coop, you didn't have a drug problem for real."

"Yeah, I know that. But Dr. Johnson told me to say that the weed interferes with me going to work. So that made it a problem. He said that's the only way I could get into this unit and into the program, so I lied!" She laughed. "Anyway girl, what I was telling you was that all he wants is to talk about my case. I told him my case has nothing to with me smoking weed. He wants to get all up in my head and I won't let him. He gets so pissed! I told Anna and Judy to watch what they say in those one on one sessions. They going to tell me, Coop, what we say to them is between us and them. I told her, girl, do you truly believe that shit? They are all the police. She said, that's what you say all the time. I told her, alright, I done told you girl, don't tell these people about your case, I am telling you. All he's doing is milking your brain. Girl, Anna didn't listen. She came to me crying. They done added another charge to her. She was in there pouring her heart out to that damn man. Now she got to go and be sentenced. I told her. She just wouldn't listen. That's what happens when you get to thinking the police is your friend. She had to learn the hard way. Now she wants to drop out and she can't because of the contract she signed. I told her just go to the class and keep your mouth shut. That's what she's been doing."

Renda said, "Damn man, that's some serious shit. Well, look I got to go in line for the shower. How are you and Pat getting along?" I told her, "On the weekends I still go get her woman for her and keep her in line for her, so she don't get caught." She said, "That's good. She felt bad about what happened." "Yeah whatever, but you know what? Commissary is necessary." She laughed and said, "Coop you're a trip."

"Let me go see can I get me a shower," I told her. I went down the hall and passed some of the girls shooting pool and on down to the first shower. I ran into Janice's officer. He said, "Man I would love to run my hands through your braids." I said, "Man, I would hate to have an assault charge on an officer." He laughed and told me, "Now Cooper you know I'm going to have you sooner or later. You might as well make it easy on yourself and make it sooner rather than later." I said, "When dogs get wings and fly. Look I didn't ask you to bring me liquor. You the one who kept bringing it to me. I am not in here for being a government prostitute. You want a cheap trick? I am not her. I just want to do my time. Why are you fucking with me anyway, man?" He looked at me and said, "Because you are a challenge, Miss Cooper."

He walked off and left me standing there. I went back to my room. There was no way in hell I was going to get in that shower at that moment. I'll wait. Yeah, I was scared. I had a feeling he was just waiting to catch me. If he was going to corner me off, it wasn't going to be tonight. I went back to my room and told Renda what happened. She said, "You know he's going to corner you, so watch out girl. Why did you braid you hair back up? It looked good permed." I said, "Because I work a lot and hey, I ain't trying to catch a man. As long as I put my makeup on so they know I'm not a shim, then it don't matter." She said, "True. Don't bite my head off! I just asked a question." I said, "I know. I'm sorry. This has just been one of those days. Damn Renda, I want to take my shower!" She said, "Come on. He's expecting you to take yours downstairs, let's go upstairs. I'll watch out for you. If he asks me, I'll tell him you're in Belinda's room or something. Come on." So I got my shower bag, PJ's and underwear and went upstairs.

I ran into Belinda's cub and decided to make peace halfway with her. We hugged and I went on to the shower. Nobody was in it. I told Renda, "Bitch don't you let them catch me. If you do I'll fuck you up in your sleep!" She said, "Oh please! Get in the shower." Renda always had my back. I had her and Reecy in my corner. I went in and had me a nice hot shower. I came out and we walked back to our room. Renda told me a story about her husband. I told her, "I still can't believe your husband robbed a bank because he thought he was going to be in the same prison with you! Girl, where did you meet this man?"

She said, "One night in a club, he bought me a beer." I said, "That figures, because I knew you two didn't meet in a church." She laughed. "Coop, I got to finish this Bible study." I said, "Yeah and I need to get some sleep. And thanks again roommate." She sad, "Yeah, you welcome now go to bed."

I got in my bed and laid there for a minute thinking about my life.

I asked myself, "What happened? God, what happened?" And then I went to sleep. Next morning after I got off from work I went to the track. I saw the officer on the perimeter track keeping up with a girl in pink spandex shorts. She was real skinny and dark. I knew right off the bat what that was about. I put my head phones on and got in step with the music. It was a lot of us on the track that day.

I was walking and singing when I spotted a helicopter overhead, then a rope dropped and this Spanish mama ran and caught it and went up in the helicopter. I said, "What the hell?" Everybody went to hollering, "You go girl! Go! Go! Go girl!" We were so happy for her! She made it! She got away! The police went to yelling, "Back to your unit! Now! All you inmates, back to your units!" Police were coming from everywhere. They were clearing the track. I was so excited to see something like that. But I didn't want the police to know I was one of the people that was on the track, so I got deep in the crowd and when I made it to the unit I changed clothes and pretended I was asleep. The girls that were working had to return to the unit.

When my roommate came in the room, she woke me up, at least she think she woke me up. She said, "Cooper, Coop girl, wake up!" I said, "What? Damn girl! What do you want?" She said, "Girl, a Spanish mama just escaped in a helicopter right there on the track! The compound is full of officers. Girl, can you believe it?"

I sat up. "Do you know who it was? What unit was she in?"

"Girl, she was in unit E-F. Hey. ain't your co-defendant in that unit?"

"Yeah," I said. She said, "Well when they let us out you should ask her about it."

"What do you mean, when they let us out?" I asked.

She said, "We're on lock down. The feds and all are here. They are questioning everybody that was on the yard. I heard that everybody that was on the track is under investigation." I said, "What? What did you just say?" She said, "Yeah everybody that was on the track. Most of them is in the SHU." I sat there looking crazy as hell. She said, "Girl, what's wrong with you? You was asleep, so why you acting like that?" I played dumb and said, "Huh? Oh, I was just thinking about what you said." She said, "Man, I can't believe this!" I got up and let her tell me everything she heard. I just listened and laughed. We stayed on lockdown for a week. They questioned everybody. Of course I stayed in the background.

A month later the Spanish mama got caught. She and her man. They were in a jewelry store buying rings. I got mad at her. She had got away. Man, I wonder what made them go to that store to buy some damn rings! That was the talk of the compound for a long time. Things calmed down and everything went back to normal. Like fights and people that turn their heads. A lot of times the officer would tell us, "Those if you who don't draw blood, don't come telling us shit." And they meant it. One day, I had been shopping and this Jamaican and African was fussing about something that I don't remember.

Anyway, the Jamaican lived in the bus stop, the rooms that were to the left of the lobby. Man, about three Africans came in that door and pulled that girl out of her room and steel-toed that girl bad. I just stood there, watching. Nobody moved. When they got through, they left. She was messed up. I couldn't believe it. And the officer was in the station on the phone. One girl walked in, it must have been her friend, because she went to screaming and crying. She went and got the officer off the phone. He called medical, and medical called the ambulance for her. That girl had broken ribs, nose, leg, and arm. I'm just happy they didn't kill her. After that, they locked up all the African girls until they told who came up in the unit and beat that girl like that. Of course, nobody ever told.

Even the girls like me, who stood there and watched the beating didn't open our mouths. Things went on as usual. One day we were at work and it was break time so all of us: me, Belinda, New York and her friend, Yada were sitting around. New York said, "Girl, I am tired of this place. I'm going to make them transfer me." I said, "How do you plan on doing this?" She said, "Right before count I'm going to show you." Then she burst out laughing. To know New York is to love her. She was sunny as hell and fear was one of the things she didn't have. That's why I like being around her. I could only imagine what she was planning to do. So after work, we did our usual thing. Go to the track and walk, go to the weight pile, then back to the unit and shower and get ready for the afternoon when all hell would break loose.

So, like one day, I am sitting watching TV and I glanced upstairs. There sat Katie. Her head was down, drooling at the mouth with her damn needle again, still stuck in her arm. I said, "Shit. I'm tired of her." She's going to get busted and then they will bring the dogs in, and I did not want to get busted with my weed. I ran upstairs and got a paper towel and took the needle out of her arm and stuck it under her bed in a pair of boots. Then I dragged her to her bed and laid her down. I closed her door and went back to watching TV. About ten minutes later her roommate was going up the steps and I told her what happened. She was hot with her. She was cursing going up the steps.

Now back to New York. That fool! Right before count, she got her commissary and climbed up on the roof and sat up there, eating. We told her, "Fool, bring your ass down. It's count time." She said, "No, no, hell no! I ain't coming down. They are going to have to come up here and get me." Now you talking about funny! It was funny as hell to watch the officer try to get New York down. When she saw them coming, she would move to another spot on the roof, dragging that damn bag. I laughed so hard my stomach was hurting! They were getting mad at her, too. They made us go in. It took them about fifteen minutes and six officers to get that nut down. It was funny as hell! New York got her wish. They put her in the SHU, and later she was shipped to Danbury FCI. Everybody was talking about New York. One of the officers told us that after they made us go in, New York started throwing her commissary at them. One officer almost fell off the roof when she hit him with a can of black beans. The girl is crazy. I missed her a lot.

About a month after that, I met this girl named Truck. She thought she was a man for real. She liked this girl in A-B unit. The girl wasn't gay. But still, she would be nice to Truck. Truck had told her she was going to be her's. If she couldn't have her, nobody was. The girl had a boyfriend. He would come visit her. Truck was jealous of the girl's man. One day they had been in the unit shooting pool and Truck told her she needed to break up with that dude because she wasn't sharing. The girl started laughing. She knew that the girl was crazy about her. Yet she kept teasing Truck. She was letting her buy her things from commissary. Her friends told her to leave that crazy girl alone. She didn't take it serious. So one day they had been playing a game of pool.

Nobody knew what was said but all they saw was Truck taking one of those little garden hoes and while the girl was lying in her bed, she beat that girl to death with it. They said that girl had over forty holes in her. Blood was everywhere. We were sitting on the patio when the feds came and took Truck. All she was saying when they was taking her was, "I told her." And she was smiling as she said it! Last I heard of Truck was that they put her behind the wall, which is where she needed to be.

Around this time I had TEAM. I hated TEAM because my

counselor and I went through this thing about my address and halfway house. Let me explain. They would ask, "Is your release address the same?" And I would say, "If they die before I'm released, release me to the nearest nursing home in the area." He would get so mad and say, "Miss Cooper, you know we have to have an address." I told him, "By the time 2032 come, my children will be having grandchildren. Most of my brothers and sisters will be dead and as for that fucking halfway house, they didn't lock my black ass halfway up, so I am not going to be let halfway out. I do not want a halfway house, so please don't talk to me about that. Please. Now is there anything else?" He said, "Yes. First you need to do something about that mouth of yours. And second, you are being transferred to Danbury FCI. So if you don't mind, go pack your shit!"

I got up and he said "Miss Cooper?" I said, "Yeah." He told me, "I am going to miss you. You are a firecracker!" I laughed and went out the door. I went to my room and started packing up my property. Everybody was asking where I was I was transferring to. A lot of the girls, including me, couldn't understand why they would transfer me while I was still in the drug program. I only had a month to go. I went back to my counselor and asked him about it. He told me that had nothing to do with it. So I went back and finished packing.

I was finishing up when my roommate came in crying. I said, "Girl what the hell is wrong with you? I am not dying, just transferring." She said, "Coop, I never had a friend like you. You accepted me just like I am. You were one roommate who didn't run off and you didn't talk about me. I never had a real friend. What am I going to do now?"

I told her, "First thing is stop snotting and going on and help me take my property to R&D. And then give me your information so we can keep in touch. You helped me when no one else would." She said, "Your co-defendant is transferring too." I told her, "I figured that much." I said, "Hey, you getting ready to go home, right" She said, "Yeah, I got another eight months." I laughed and said, "Shit! You were going to leave here anyway. What kind of stuff is that? It's alright for you to leave me, but you don't want me to leave you."

She stopped crying and started laughing. She said, "Coop you make me sick. Still, I don't want you to transfer." "Well, I said "Tell them you don't want to me go." Then I said, "Oh, but I do want to go. It's time for me to move on. I've been here over a year. All this time I got, I need to move around so my time won't be so hard on me. You are getting ready to go home to your children. I don't know when I'm going to see my kids again. By the time I get out of here, my baby will be a middle aged woman with grandkids. So you see what I mean, right?"

She was quiet, then, "When you leave?" I told her, "I don't know. I've never transferred before. Come on and help me with this stuff." Renda and I took my property down to R&D, the place I came into when I got to this prison a year ago. It seemed so strange. So I sat while the man packed my stuff and marked off each item. And when he finished, he handed me a sheet with everything I own. I learned that it is called a form forty. We left R&D and went back to the unit. I went to use the phone to tell my family that I was being moved. My mama answered on the first ring. I said, "Hey madear." She said, "Baby, how you doing? I am so glad you called me." She asked, "What's wrong? Did something happen?" I said, "No, madear. I'm just calling to tell you that they are moving me to another prison." She said, "Oh baby, where they sending you now?" I told her I was going to Danbury, Connecticut.

She said, "That's still far away. Why can't they send you closer? I miss you baby." I said, "I miss you too. Madear have you heard from Shon? Has he called you?" She said, "Yeah, he doing okay. He said he had to become a man real quick. He had asked about you, too. He worries about you." I said, "I worry about him, too. How's Nita and Alexis?" She said, "Alexis got in trouble in the lunch line." I told mama, "It's my fault." My sweet mama said, "No baby, it's not your fault. It's that mans fault. I wish you had never had any dealings with him." I said, "But madear, before all this happened, you said he was a good man and now that I'm in prison, it's his fault."

"Yeah." she said, "But it is his fault. You never sold that stuff."

"It's okay, madear. Alexis is just mad at the world right now. But she will be okay. How's Nita and her new husband?"

"She's okay. She wants to come get her little sister when spring breaks." "That's good. At the moment, all they have is each other. Well my mama I'm going to let you go for now. I love you lady."

"I love you to, my baby." I hung up the phone.

When I went back to my room, my roommate told me the officer wanted to see me. I went to see what he wanted. He said, "Cooper, since you're in the drug program, they decided not to ship you. But your co-defendant is still leaving. R&D is closed. But tomorrow morning you need to go and get your property."

I said, "Man, I just called and told my mama I was being shipped. Now I'm going to have to go and tell her that I'm not being shipped." He said, "You going to be shipped, Miss Cooper, just not now. You have four weeks left in the program, and then you will be leaving." I said, "Okay. Thank you." He said, "You're welcome. It's not so bad, Cooper." I just left and went back to my room to tell bunkie that I would be her roommate another month.

When I got to my room, my roommate was getting ready to cook. I said, "Whatcha cooking?" She said, "I thought I would fix us some Chilla Keta, fried rice and a cheesecake." I said, "Are you fixing us something or are you having a party?" She said, "No girl, this is for us and we can eat off this the whole weekend." I said, "Yeah, I didn't think about that. Look while you're doing that, I am going over to E-F unit and see if I can find Mattie."

I left and went outside to walk over to the E-F unit. There was a couple of people standing outside. So I asked them if they knew

Mattie. One said yes. I asked her if she didn't mind to tell Mattie that I was outside. She said, "What's your name?" I told her and she said, "Okay" and I thanked her. Then she went in. I stood outside and lit myself a cigarette. She came back out and told me Mattie was coming. When Mattie came, I told her that I wasn't leaving until I finish the program. She said, "Oh, okay. I was wondering about that. It didn't seem right for them to ship you while you were in the drug program." "Yeah," I said. "Anyway, my counselor said I would be here another month. So when are you leaving?" She said, "Monday morning. I'll be gone when you come to R&D to get your property. But I'll be waiting on you." I said, "Mattie, I am going to miss you. We have come a long way together, huh?" She said, "Sure have, girlfriend."

Then, for the first time in a long time, I thought about Niecy Doll. I asked Mattie "Where did they send Niecy Doll." She said, "Girl, I thought you knew. Niecy Doll went to do her state time first." I said, "How much state does she have?"

"Five years, but she won't do no more than two and a half."

"Good. So Mattie, what are we going to do your last weekend here?"

"Nothing special. I really don't want to go but it will be a good change."

"Yeah, I don't want to go either, but hey, it ain't like they asked us!" "Yeah you're right," she laughed. I said, "Anyway, have my care package ready for me when I get there." She said, "I got you.

When was the last time you talked to my sister, Linda?" I told her a couple of weeks ago. She told me she called her yesterday and Linda told her she had talked to Diamond. He told her he had sent me some money. I said, "Is that right? Did he send me a ticket home?" She said, "I don't think he's able to do that." I laughed and said, "Alright Mattie. You take care. See you in Danbury." I left her and went to the track. I decided do me a quick two miles and head back to the unit.

Out on the track while walking, I was doing some thinking. I was thinking, "Was what I did so bad that I deserved forty years? I mean, I didn't kill anyone, and I didn't sell drugs. I didn't do anything, Lord. Why did You take me away from my kids? Why did You let them send my son to a penitentiary, a USP? Lord, why? I just don't understand why! Lord, I know You're there, so why don't You answer me? What kind of God are You?" I left the track and went back to my unit. He just was not serving me any kind of purpose at all. At least that's what I thought at the time.

When I got to my unit, I went and sat in front of the TV. The rule with the TV was, if you were first to get in the lobby and had the remote, then you controlled the TV. If you get up and go outside and somebody comes behind you, then they got control and you have to watch what they watch on TV. So at the moment I was in control of the TV. Everybody had to watch what I watched on TV. I sat there a couple of hours and when one of the girls came and sat down, I gave the remote to her. I went to see if my roommate had finished cooking.

She was at the microwave. When she looked up and saw me, she said, "Coop, where have you been? I was about to put an APB out on you. I'm through. You ready to eat?" "Yeah," I said. "That's why I came looking for you." She said, "Come on, let's eat." Then Belinda came up. She said, "Coop, you going to the skating ring?" I told her, "Yeah. I'm going just to watch you try to show out and fall on your fat ass." Renda laughed and said, "Yeah, she be trying to show out for her woman." Belinda said, "Man, you all ain't got to talk about me like that. I know that I can't skate that good. And Cooper, I don't know why you're laughing, you can't skate at all!" So I said, "I'm still going so I can watch you bust your ass." Belinda said, "Whatever," and left.

My bunkie and I went back to the room and ate. Then I went and ironed my jeans and took off to the skating ring. Before I could get out the door, Janice came and asked me did I have anything. I told her, "Girl, I packed out today. I'm sorry girlfriend, I ain't got nothing!" Half of them in there were high. I spotted Belinda and her girlfriend. I saw Reecy and her little girlfriend. She saw me and came over. She said, "Hey Coop, I hear you packed out. When do you leave?" I said, "Not for another month. I'm in the drug program, so I'm here for now." She said, "What about Mattie?" I told her, "Mattie leaves on Monday, which is good for me, because she'll have everything ready for me when I get there." She said, "Yeah, I guess it is. Don't leave without hollering at me, okay friend?" I told her, "I will let you know a day before, I promise."

Her girlfriend never said a word while Niecy Doll and I talked. I knew it was because she was scared of Niecy Doll. She would beat the brakes off her women. All of them were like trained puppies. And all in all, I had a good time that night. Mattie and her gang were there. After they called compound closed, we all went back to our units. It was a late night which means we can stay up until two thirty in the morning. After count, I went and took my shower and got me a pillow and a blanket and camped out on the sofa and watched TV. After two o'clock count, I got up and went to bed. I was off on Sunday and Monday. That Monday morning, I went and got my property. I put all my stuff back in order and things went on as always.

One night, Pat went into labor. All that day she was in labor and the officer had to deliver the baby. He looked scared. Officer Johnson had us scared. All he kept saying was, "Push!" He said he wasn't a damn doctor. They had called for an ambulance. It seemed to be taking forever. I was standing outside the door when I heard the officer say, "Damn, I see the head! Alright, now push hard." She did and the baby came out. He told one of the girls to "Hand me…" then I heard the baby cry. About ten minutes later, the men from the ambulance came and took Pat and her baby boy to the hospital. Mr. Johnson was proud of himself. He said, "I got to go call my wife and tell her about this." We were laughing at him. That was the talk of the compound for about a week.

One day on my way to drug class, Belinda came hollering,

"Cooper, girl, guess what? Mr. Taylor shot Shona!"

I said, "Girl, go ahead with that."

She said, "For real! He and another officer was taking her to an outside doctor. That nut tried to run and Mr. Taylor shot her!"

I said, "Oh my God! Did he kill her?"

She said, "No, he shot her in the butt. They are laying him off for two weeks."

I said, "What about her?"

She said, "Right now, she's in the hospital. But you know she is going to be shipped as soon as possible. Hey, did you hear about Mr. Thomas?"

I said, "No I didn't and if you are going to tell me then you are going to walk and talk at the same time because I'm late for class."

She said, "Come on. I'll walk with you. Now you know Judy and Mr. Thomas be going at it like it's legal. He be working double shifts and everything so he can be around her."

I said, "Yeah so…"

She said, "Well Judy got sick and went to medical and medical didn't see her. They sent her back to the unit. So Mr. Thomas came and went up to her room. The next thing we know, he comes down the steps with Judy in his arms walking cross the compound taking her to medical. They had told him to stay out of that unit and he still goes in there. Well, now they are shipping Judy and Mr. Thomas resigned."

"Girl, you are lying."

She said, "No I ain't."

I said, "Damn! I just can't believe this shit, just like that."

"Yeah, man. Well look I'll talk to you later. I can't believe it, now that's deep."

I went on to class. The doctor and I went through the same thing. He said I needed to open up. Like I told him before, "My case, to me, had nothing to do with this class." I made it through another one. Class was finished. On my way back to my unit, I hear my name called. "Inmate Cooper, report to your unit to see your counselor." Now I'm wondering, "What now?" So I got to my unit and when I walk to his office he said to me, "Cooper, report to R&D with your property." I said, "What?"

He said, "I know, but they said you had to go to Danbury now."

I said, "Who said I had to go?"

"Cooper, please just take your property. Please. I am not a bad guy. OK?"

"Yeah whatever," I said, and then I left.

I went and started packing out again. I had just done this three weeks ago. And here I go again. I was halfway through when Renda walked in and said, "Hi Bunkie, what's up?"

I said, "What do you think? I'm packing out again. I have to go to R&D with my property."

"What? NO! They said you wouldn't leave until you finish the program."

I said, "Well I got to go. Are you going to help me or what? Come on."

She pouted and said, "Yeah, I'm going to help you." So we finished with my property and took it on a cart to R&D. It was the same officer that was in there the last time. He said, "Well, are you going to make it this time?" I said, "Of course I am, and I know why." He smiled and said, "Why?? I said, "Because I don't want to go, that's why. I know I'm going."

He laughed. "Well, come on. Go bring me those boxes and let's pack you out. You put them in the box and I'll check them off." He looked at Renda and asked, "Who are you?" Renda said, "I'm her roommate." He said, "Ok, you take them out and hand them to her." She packed while I wrote. He said, "How many socks?" It went on like that until we were through. When we finished, we went back toward the track. We walked and talked about everything and nothing. I was really going to miss Renda. We went back to the unit, and on our way everybody kept asking, "Cooper did you pack out today?" "Yeah," I would tell them. Then I remembered I had to find Reecy to tell her I was leaving. I found her in the barn playing basketball. She looked up and saw me. She came over and I told her, "Hey friend I'm leaving again." She said, "Damn Coop, I am going to miss you. Take care until we run into each other again. I know we will, so I'll just say see you later." I laughed and said, "Later," and turned around and went out the door. I went back to the track and started walking. I had to get to myself and think.

Lord, I didn't want to go to another prison. I wanted to go home. I started crying. I was tired. I wanted to be with my kids. I knew it wasn't going to happen. But still, I wanted to see a family member, any family member. A brother, sister, or nephew. It didn't matter, I was homesick. After I got over myself, I walked back to the unit. I had decided I wasn't going to call home. I mean, for what? I was on my own, by myself. I told myself, "strap up girlfriend. You are about to become a snow bunny." I went to the unit and I got some soap and lotion from my bunkie because my silly behind packed out everything I own. We stayed up late laughing half the night. Then here comes Janice's friend, the officer. He said, "Miss Cooper, I hear you have packed out. Is that true?"

"Why?" I asked. "Why do you want to know?"

He said, "You don't answer a question with a question. Did you pack out today?"

I answered him, "Yes. I did."

He grabbed me by my hair and said, "Well then I guess I'll see you tomorrow night, Miss Cooper." He let my hair go and smiled at me and left. Renda said, "Roommate, he's planning on getting you tomorrow night." I said, "In his dreams. He ain't getting shit from me. Look, I'm going to bed. I'll see you in the morning, since I don't have to go to work." She said, "Ok, good night Bunkie." I told her to sleep with the angels.

About four a.m. an officer came and woke me up and told me to get dressed, I was leaving. I didn't wake Renda up. The kitchen workers were already up and dressed. When they saw me come down the hall they said, "Coop you leaving?" I said, "Yeah, I got to go out with you all. Then I looked up and there was Renda, crying. Talking about, "Why didn't you wake me up?" I said, "Because I knew you were going to cry." She hugged me and said, "I love you Coop. Take care of yourself and don't ever forget me." I said, "How could I? You put your photo in the Bible, remember?" She smiled and said, "Oh yeah. See you friend." I walked out with the kitchen workers and the officer walked me to R&D. They dressed me out and handcuffed and black boxed me.

The feds took me to the airlift. I was at the airfield and saw all these people with their guns. I got on the plane. I already knew not to drink anything because I would have to use the bathroom. They took me to Oklahoma. When I got there, they dressed us out in these red jumpsuits. Well, when they asked for our underwear I refused to give mine up. They were going to give me used underwear! I wasn't going to do it, so they put me in lockdown. Cut the air on me and took my sheet. I had a wool blanket and a pillow. That was it. I didn't care. I was not going to wear used underwear. Everybody else who was supposed to leave on the airlift to Danbury had left. I was still freezing my butt off in Oklahoma. I stayed there for two weeks.

One day they was counting and the officer asked me, "Who are you?" I said, "Dianne Cooper." He looked on his list and said, "Number?" I told him, "08087-021." He said, "You're not here." He left and came back. He asked me, "How long have you been here?" I told him, "Almost two weeks." He left again. About an hour later he came back and said, "You're not in our system. Where did you come from?" I said, "Pleasanton, California." He left. I didn't see him anymore that day. The next day a different officer came. He said, "Cooper, Dianne, 08787-021." I said, "Yes?" He said, "Pack up. Let's go." I got my stuff. He opened my door and I walked out ahead of him. He took me in this little room. A lady officer came and dressed me out. A fed lady came in. Handcuffed me, shackled me and put me in a van. They had one man in there.

We went to the airport and got on the airlift again. We flew to Danbury. They put me in a van. It was me and two other girls, Terry and Gloria. We became friends fast. When we got to Danbury, I was the last one to get off the van. When I got off, the officer said, "Miss. Cooper?" I said, "Yes." She said, "We've been waiting on you! Where have you been?" I said, "Lost in the system!"

Group Discussion Guide for

Dark Justice

1. Dianne refuses to cooperate with the authorities throughout the book. She states that she would never tell on her family, even at the risk of being incarcerated for forty years. Would you have done the same? Why or why not?

2. Dianne mentions more than once that Diamond loves her and she loves him. In light of Diamond's actions prior to and after his subsequent arrest, such as using her car for nefarious reasons, sending her to pick up his money or drugs, and finally lying in court for his own benefit, do you believe that he truly loved her?

3. There are several instances where Dianne claims that she was "green" for example, not knowing that her son was selling drugs, not recognizing drugs, etc. Do you believe that Dianne was in fact an innocent or that naïve? If so, why? If not, why not?

4. While on her cruise vacation, Dianne states that she only attracts drug dealers. Do you think this statement is a reflection of a lack of self esteem or a reason to excuse her own attraction to these types of men?

5. In Chapter 3, Dianne finds out that her son, Shon, has been selling drugs. When she asks him why, he states: "They put my daddy on crack, so I'm putting their daddy on crack." Do you think this is a valid reason to sell drugs? What would you have said to your child if you were in this situation?

For more information about the author or to schedule appearances or order additional copies of Dark Justice, please visit:
www.wildivypublishing.com/authordiannecooper

Turn the page for a sneak preview of

Dark Justice 2
Searchin'

Coming Summer, 2016

Here I am again. My name is Cooper. I'm the one who has been traveling around the world with the Bureau of Prisons! They have just transferred me from Dublin, California, also known as Pleasanton. They lost me in the system. Can you believe that? All the while I was in an Oklahoma Detention Center, freezing my butt off all because I refused to wear someone else's used panties.

Two weeks after they found me, here I sit in R&D Danbury. Myself and the two girls that was on the van with me. I don't think I'm going to like it here. Listen at me! As if I have a choice. Talking about I don't think I'm going to like it here. Nobody cares if I like it here or not. An officer says, "Cooper?"

"Yeah?"

"Come on. I got to take you to laundry."

We walk out to R&D and I stop... SNOW! And then I continue to look around me. It wasn't much to see. I mean it is a complete circle. I said, "This it? This is all of the compound?" He laughed and said, "Oh it's bigger than it looks." I said, "Oh for real? You could have fooled me!" We went to laundry. I got my bedding, uniforms, tee shirts, socks, underwear, boots and a jacket. I put it all in my laundry bag and he told me I was in unit five. He took me to my unit and gave me my cubicle number. I went to my cubicle and there lying on her bed was Tracy. I put my stuff on the chair and started making my bed, while Tracy stood there sizing me up. As I made my bed I was thinking to myself, "Yeah, whatever you're thinking, stop. You think long and you're going to think wrong. Please don't try me." She had gotten up and was just standing, there watching me. Finally, she said, "Hey. What's your name?" I stopped tying my sheet and turned to face her. I said, "My name is Cooper, not 'hey you.' What's yours?" She said, "Look, all I asked you was your name, so let's not get off on the wrong foot here, okay? I mean you are moving in my cub so don't come in here all smart mouthed and shit."

I just looked at this piece of nothing and said, "Lady, you don't know anything about me and I don't know and don't *want* to know anything about you. I can promise you this, I won't be your roommate for very long. I can see you don't want me in here and I am damn sure I don't want to be here. I am tired. I've had a bad day. All I want to do is make this bed and find my co-defendant and use the phone." She said, "So who is your co-defendant?" I said, "Mattie Jones. You know her?" She said, "Big, red lady? Yea, I know her. She works in the kitchen and lives in Unit One for long timers." She looked at me again and then she said, "You must don't have a lot of time." I said, "Oh yeah, I got a lot of time." She said, "What do you call a lot of time? You wouldn't be over here if you had more than ten years."

I said, "Lady, I have a forty year life sentence. Is that enough time for you?" All she could say was "Oh Shit! You lying! I am so sorry Cooper. I didn't know, man. Why did they give you all that? Look, finish your bed and I'm going to find Miss Mattie and let her know you're here." She wasn't gone five minutes when she said, "Hey Coop, when I stepped out the door, Miss Mattie was on her way over here. She's outside waiting on you." I said, "Okay, thank you." She said, "Coop, look we kind of got off on the wrong foot. Let's start over."

"Sure. No problem."

I went out the door and Mattie stood there, smiling. "I've been waiting on you! What happened?"

I said, "Girl, it's a long story. I'll tell you about it."

She said, "So look, I already got it set up with my counselor. You will be moving over here with me."

I said, "Good." She told me to come go with her. I walked over to her unit. I asked her, "Where is the officer's station?"

She said, "Girl the officers only come over here when we have mail call and count. The only other time we see an officer is when we call them." She pointed to the phone on the wall and said, "Call them on the phone."